Touched by the M

Bonus Photos and Stories

Dave Combs

FREE BONUS BOOKLET

To thank you for purchasing and reading my book,
I am going to give you a free color bonus booklet. In it you will find
lots of color photos from my childhood and later.
I expand on some of the stories in this book with maybe a story
or two not in this book.

To get your free bonus booklet, go to this link:
https://CombsMusic.com/bonusbooklet

TOUCHED BY THE MUSIC

Brilliantly written, Dave Combs' book *Touched by the Music*, is as beautiful, engaging and inspiring as his world renowned music. This is a story about love and relationships, perseverance and tenacity and one man's journey to bring joy, comfort and peace to millions through his incredible music. It is about a life beautifully orchestrated by his love of God and his genuine heartfelt desire to share his gifts with others. Few of us have the opportunity to enhance the lives of so many like my friend Dave Combs. His music and his message will live forever.

One final thought – for those who have listened to and been moved by "Rachel's Song" you are going to absolutely love this book – for those new to Dave's music and his endearingly authentic writing -something special is about to happen.

—**BERRY FOWLER,**
Founder, Sylvan Learning Centers and
Fowler International Academy of Professional Coaching

Somehow Dave overheard God's eternal 'music of the spheres.' Sliding onto his piano bench, he dashed off 'Rachel's Song,' capturing the harmony of the human heart with all its pathos and ecstasy. The business of this book is the incredible account of what happened next!

—**DAN GRIFFIN,**
DMin, Pastor Emeritus, Cliff Temple Baptist Church, Dallas, TX

Listening to Dave's music and reading his book, most specifically the myriad letters of gratitude he has received, the word that jumps out at me is "peace". Notice how frequently his fans write of that blessing—one that is so prominently referred to in scripture. He has helped bring peace to tens of thousands of people—through who he is, certainly through his music, and now through his written words. How has he done this? Well, it is truly a "peace that passeth all understanding." With tens of thousands of others, I thank you, Dave. And God bless you.

—**MARK JACOBY,**
Actor, Singer, Performer,
Leading roles on Broadway including *Show Boat*,
The Phantom of the Opera, and *Ragtime*

Having known Dave most of my live, I am personally aware of his love of music. We grew up together in church, scouts, and explorers, as well as school. Music has always been a vital part of his life and personality.

When I first heard "Rachel's Song," like so many others, I was 'touched' by the beauty and calmness it offered without knowing why. After reading Dave's revealing story, *Touched by the Music*, his song takes on new meaning. You will be moved by the journey of "Rachel's Song" from Dave's heart to a powerful melody of God's love expressed through music. You will be "touched" as so many others have as you hear their stories of life-changing encounters with this song. You will never hear this song again in the same way once you read the story behind it and be doubly blessed as once again you are "touched by the music."

—CARLOS PETERSON,
DMin, Retired Pastor

In 1989 while driving my car in Perth, Australia I heard a hauntingly beautiful piano piece on the radio that prompted me to stop the car and call the station to find out what it was. "Rachel's Song" immediately became part of my performance repertoire. Two years later when I recorded my first CD for Sony Music, "Rachel's Song" was Track One on the CD.

It wasn't until I began performing in the USA in the mid 1990's that I discovered the amazing story of how "Rachel's Song" came to be. Now, after many phone conversations with Dave and reading "Touched by the Music," to know how this piece of music has had such an incredible effect on the lives of so many people throughout the world, is a blessing. Thank you, Dave for sharing your *"Rachel's Song" journey.*

After a church performance I did in Dallas many years ago I received an email saying … "Thank you for the message you gave us through your fingers". I didn't realize as a pianist I could minister with only the piano. Instrumental music *enters the soul, then we are no longer in control.* Thank you, Dave for following God's destiny for you and giving us music to touch and enter our souls.

—BARRY TOGNOLINI,
Pianist and Recording Artist

Touched by the Music

How the Story and Music
of "Rachel's Song"
Can Change Your Life

Dave Combs

TBTM
PUBLISHING

WINSTON-SALEM, NORTH CAROLINA

To my wife, Linda, for her inspiration, patience, advice, and love

Cover Design by: LinTaylor™ Marketing Group
Interior Design by: Thomas Nery
Published by: TBTM Publishing
Winston-Salem, North Carolina

Library of Congress Control Number: 2021917737

ISBN: Paperback: 978-1-7378263-0-9

Printed in the United States of America

TABLE OF CONTENTS

FOREWORD

Throughout my life I have had the privilege of meeting and mentoring many exceptional people. One of those people is Dave Combs. When I first met Dave, I quickly discovered what an extraordinary human being he is. Not only is he the composer of some of the most beautiful music I have ever heard, but he is a man of faith and has the heart of someone wanting to make a difference in this world. And he is a great storyteller and writer. He and I just connected on so many levels.

When I first learned about Dave and his song, "Rachel's Song," I went online and found that it was on Spotify, Pandora, iTunes, Amazon and all these places, I thought, Wow! It's an incredible song. Now that you are reading this, the first thing you've got to do is go and purchase the song on Apple iTunes or someplace like that and listen to it. It's beautiful, beautiful, beautiful music. When I first heard it, I played it twice in a row. It's the kind of thing once you hear it, you want to hear it again. I often use it in my seminars as people are coming into the room in the morning to set the right tone for the day. It's a beautiful piece of music.

One of my passions in life is to teach. I started my professional career as a high school history teacher. I continue to be a teacher by nature. I love helping motivated individuals find their best life. I learned so much in the course of co-writing and marketing the *Chicken Soup for the Soul®* series of books culminating in perhaps my most challenging book, *The Success Principles™: How to Get from Where You Are to Where You Want to Be*. To teach these tried-and-true principles, I have been hosting for years what I call my Mastermind Retreats. For the participants, these have been life-changing events.

It was at one of those retreats that I met and got to know Dave. Over the course of the three days that I spent with Dave I read his new book, *Touched by the Music: How the story and music of "Rachel's Song" can change your life*. In addition to being a gifted composer, Dave is also an entrepreneur and has created a successful music business. One of the things that is beautiful about this book, in addition to his song and the music he has created, is that it really is a primer in what to do if you want to get something out into the world. It's about trusting your intuition, taking action, not giving up, being persistent and consistent—all principles I talk about all the time. Throughout his book I realized how much of Dave's journey with his music parallels the principles that are in my *The Success Principles*™ book.

A good example of the principle of taking action is the story I love about how Dave was in Nashville and got "Rachel's Song" recorded. He tells how he just left his hotel one night and said, "Well, I'll just go and find where they record music." And he drove down to the area in Nashville called Music Square. Nearly all the places were closed, but he found one. Dave talked to the man in that studio, and he told him about another studio across the street that was exactly what he was looking for. As a result of that Dave got connected with Gary Prim, the very talented studio musician, who arranged and performed "Rachel's Song" for the recording.

Another example is how the Law of Attraction kicked in for Dave after "Rachel's Song" got recorded. Dave told me how his vision for creating soothing, relaxing music and sharing it with people all over the world dominated his thoughts, talk, beliefs, and feelings—all key elements of the Law of Attraction. That vision has now materialized. He has written over 110 songs, has 15 albums of music, and 11 piano music books. This didn't happen overnight, but it did happen, and in this book Dave talks about how he did it—how he was able to sell his music all over the United States. And here's another interesting part to me—with no advertising.

One thing about Dave's book that I love is that the stories he tells are phenomenal—but the other part is he's a really good writer. I couldn't stop turning the pages. I know you are going to enjoy reading these fascinating stories because the stories are just as inspiring as "Rachel's Song" is musically inspiring. And again, make sure you get a copy of "Rachel's Song" by going to your favorite online music source, whatever that is. Download it to your computer or your cell phone and play it. I promise you'll find it is really, really very inspiring and very comforting music. I recommend you play it as you start to read this book. Let this book and "Rachel's Song" serve as your launching pad to being inspired and *Touched by the Music*.

~Jack Canfield,
Coauthor of the *Chicken Soup for the Soul*® series and
The Success Principles™: *How to Get from Where You Are to Where You Want to Be*

INTRODUCTION

Can a simple song with no words have the power to change your life? Yes, it can. It did for me, and it has for countless others like yourself. My story begins with one song, *Rachel's Song*, which has touched millions of lives and still counting. This book and my music can elevate your joy and bring you peace through the power of soft, soothing, relaxing music and inspirational stories.

Speaking of bringing peace, one of the first stories I received was from a trained EMT who had stopped her car to help an elderly man that she saw clutch his chest and collapse on the sidewalk. When she reached the gentleman, she saw that he was breathing much too fast out of fear. And from her car radio, "Rachel's Song" just happened to be playing. She yelled to her husband, "Turn that music up loud!" as she comforted the old man by having him listen to the heavenly lullaby-like song. By the time the song finished, the man had calmed down. And by then a doctor had come from a near-by office to further care for him. She later tracked down the name of the song and my address from the radio station and sent the story to me in a letter.

I still find it amazing that one piece of music, with a simple melody and no words—could have such a profound effect.

This book—and being *touched by the music*—extends beyond the creation of "Rachel's Song," which you will learn about shortly. The stories in this book illustrate what happened when I tuned into God's sacred timing and listened to His voice. My stories reveal some of the small (and big) "miracles" God provided—in day-to-day moments. And stories from others reinforce the joy and encouragement delivered through inspired music.

The significance of some of these important moments seemed invisible to my naked eye. Only by listening to Him did I later see how He orchestrated their purpose. One of those moments was the creation of "Rachel's Song." When I first played the song, I remember feeling as if I were simply playing a beautiful and emotionally moving song that had existed for many years. It never occurred to me that I was "writing" a song. Looking back, I realize that the song had to be inspired—a gift from God. Thanks to the encouragement of my wonderful wife, Linda, I answered His call to share this music with the world, touching all who hear it.

The decision to write this book was the result of another encouragement from Linda. Encouragement is but one of her many endearing qualities. At programs for churches and civic organizations, she and I experienced first-hand the motivational and inspirational impact of sharing the many personal stories about my journey with my music.

In preparation for writing this book, I re-read many of the thousands of notes and letters I have received over the years. I was again moved to tears, as these individuals poured out their hearts and bared their souls with stories of what "Rachel's Song" meant to them. They shared how "Rachel's Song" made them feel—at peace, calm, close to God. One person wrote, "Your music is the closest thing to *angel music* I have ever heard." Others told me the song was played at their wedding, birth of their child, or passing of a loved one—making those moments more joyful, bearable, endearing. Some even said it took away physical pain—or started lifelong relationships or saved their lives. Their emotions ranged from pure joy to deep sorrow, and everything in between—but all with an expression of how the music uplifted them. A selection of these special stories can be found in Chapter 21. You will also find a short, heart-warming quote from a fan at the beginning of each chapter.

It is my hope that you will enjoy my stories—of how a song went from creation to worldwide recognition, and how long-lasting momentum began with that tune. From writing the music of "Rachel's Song" on my old piano in my basement in 1981, to owning the copyrights to nearly 200 more songs and arrangements and having them heard by millions all over the world, is quite a journey with so much to tell. You'll read my stories of inspiration, success, rejection, confirmation, entrepreneurship, and to quote a phrase from author Squire Rushnell, "Godwinks."

It is my greater hope that you will be inspired—to welcome something greater, to receive the gift that beautiful music delivers as it washes over you, to be truly *touched by the music*.

I'm often asked, "What is the inspiration behind your music?" The short answer is: it is the joy and peace that I experience while creating the music, and knowing that this same *joy and peace* is experienced by all who hear it. It is my mission to spread my music to an ever-expanding audience, giving listeners everywhere *joy and peace*. I believe that God knew that I would be able—with His help and the help of an ever-widening circle of supporters—to spread my music around the world, to touch and bless the lives of millions.

I hope that by the time you've finished this book, you too will be blessed—knowing what it means to be *touched by the music*.

At the risk of sounding too commercial, you will likely enjoy and appreciate this book even more if you listen to the music from the album as you read. If you are not already familiar with "Rachel's Song," feel free to access CombsMusic.com to get your own CD or download. You can also stream the music online from your favorite online music source.

Are you ready to be *touched by the music*?

CHAPTER ONE

LET THE SONG BEGIN

"'Rachel's Song' is the most beautiful music I've heard in a long time.
It allows the soul to feel."
~MARY

God's Gift

When I sat down at my freshly tuned grand piano, little did I know that the next notes I played would change my life forever—and touch the hearts of millions worldwide.

I clearly remember that cool evening back in January 1981. I had just finished tuning my 100-year-old Knabe baby grand piano—a common task for me, because of its advanced age. After tuning, I'd always play something immediately, so I could enjoy the clear, beautiful sounds of the newly tuned instrument.

On this occasion, my fingers began playing in the key of C. Every note and chord I heard inside my head seemed to flow effortlessly through me and onto the keys. This may sound strange, but it felt as if the piano and I were conversing. Yet rather than me simply playing a song of my own creation, it was as if my fingers were a mere conduit—expressing the music of another master composer.

Instead of questioning where the music was coming from, I continued. After playing the first eight bars, I repeated them. Then a chorus starting with an F chord came to me—again, naturally, as if I were playing a song that I'd heard a hundred times before.

At no time did the thought cross my mind that I had just "written a song." The tune came to me as if it had always existed; I was simply expressing it for the first time.

I believe wholeheartedly that the song I played that night was not mine. Rather, it was a gift from God. For some reason I may never know—but have been blessed by ever since—He chose *me* to play it for the first time.

A few days later, my wife, Linda, came home from work. As she walked into the house, I heard her humming a tune. "What's the name of this song?" she asked me, as it continued to play from her lips. "I can't get it out of my head."

"That tune? It doesn't have a name," I said.

"What do you mean it doesn't have a name? You play it all the time on the piano," she insisted.

"It's just something I made up," I explained.

Sometimes, I would just let my fingers explore the keyboard while "messing around," as my mama used to call it. Until Linda asked me the name of the tune, it had never occurred to me that I had *written a song*.

"No, like I said, it doesn't have a name," I repeated.

Linda implored me, "Well, you better write it down. You might get hit by a truck, and this music would be lost forever!" She knew me well. If a song hadn't been named, it probably also hadn't been written down in any way that another person could play later. Music, for me, was almost a sacred experience—and the logistics of how it got created or written down were less important to me than its existence, and the effect it may have on others, including myself.

At Linda's urging—since I love my wife, and she often knows what's best when it comes to these sorts of things—I wrote out the melody and chords. If it was something she liked enough to ask me about it, then she deserved to have it on paper. "Now if something ever happens to me, you'll know where to find it," I assured her, as I placed the newly written music in the piano bench.

Here is the song exactly as I wrote it down:

Original Handwritten Music (Lead Sheet) for Rachel's Song

Over the next three years, work kept me too busy to give that lone melody much thought. As a traveling consultant with AT&T, my job kept me busy—and often on the road—working with plant managers to implement a computer system that would ultimately make their factories more efficient. I enjoyed the work, so I didn't mind the attention it took. If I could help a factory operate more effectively, I felt a strong sense of satisfaction and purpose.

But music always played within my head, even as I went about my day. And the song I'd been blessed to play on that otherwise uneventful night continued to live on.

In fact, I played that simple tune often, occasionally even sharing it with friends. But I had no idea what I was supposed to do with this special gift God had handed me. While my handwritten music stayed in my piano bench for nearly three years, in between work meetings and daily tasks, I felt stirred when I contemplated that song—and the way it came about. There was something about that song that made it stand apart from anything else I'd played in my many years of appreciating and creating music.

> **What should I be doing with this special song, which I had the privilege to play for the first time?**

What should I be doing with this special song, which I had the privilege to play for the first time? I'd allow myself to wonder on occasion.

I knew that the song was special; I just didn't know how special.

Perhaps He will reveal the answer to my question in time, I'd reassure myself before heading about my day.

The Tune Gets Its Name

In September of 1983, I learned that some very dear friends had given birth to a beautiful baby girl. Fall had already started to work its magic, igniting the trees with brilliant colors as the night air turned chilly. Growing up with the mostly deciduous trees of the mountains of East Tennessee, I always loved the fall.

The full symphony of the changing seasons came to a crescendo when our friends asked Linda and me if we would serve as the godparents of their precious angel, Rachel. Honored and humbled, we accepted.

Rachel was christened in December 1983 at a private service in her mother's home church. As Linda and I entered the small sanctuary, my gaze immediately leapt to the grand piano sitting at the front center of the church. Linda and I slipped into a pew behind the family, as we listened with wonder to the minister's words of blessing and thanksgiving for Rachel. While I held onto the minister's words, my eyes still kept drifting to the grand piano just behind him.

After the formal christening service ended, a thought occurred to me, and I felt inspired. Leaning over to Linda, I whispered into her ear.

"What do you think about me playing my song on the piano?" I asked, using her as my most trusted advisor.

She smiled and nodded her approval.

After I got the go-ahead from Linda, I asked Rachel's parents what they thought. After all, we were there for the christening of their dear child, not an impromptu concert from her godfather. Fortunately, they readily accepted my offer.

As I approached the piano, everyone sat back down in their pews.

As soon as my fingers touched the keys, something special occurred, which I wouldn't fully realize until later. My fingers floated across the keys, as the song that God placed inside of me spilled out once again. Each note seemed to lift my vision and thoughts to the miraculous new life that we were celebrating and consecrating.

It wasn't until the last note faded that I realized that tears were streaming down my face. As I rose from the piano bench and started to return to Linda's side, I noticed everyone in the room wiping tears of their own. It became clear that I wasn't the only one touched by the music that day.

Then my eyes fell on little Rachel in the arms of her mother, surrounded by her adoring family.

"From now on," I announced, "this will be known as 'Rachel's Song' in her honor." Her parents beamed their approval.

For the first time, the tune I had played at home and for a few friends had a name, and it seemed the perfect fit. God had answered my question about "what to do with this song."

Or so I thought. What I didn't realize at the time was that this was only the beginning of His plan for "Rachel's Song." There would be much more to come....

Moments That Matter Most

Music didn't just come to me in adulthood, out of the blue. I grew up with music close to my heart at all times.

From a young age, I learned how to tune musical instruments, starting with my Grandma Combs' autoharp. Whenever we'd visit her home in Virginia, she'd hand me the instrument with the expectation that I'd get it sounding as perfectly as it could.

Tuning isn't hard, but it does require practice and a good ear. I started tuning by playing one note, an A—the one that matched the pitch of my A tuning fork, since that is the only one I had. Then I sounded the tuning fork by striking it on my kneecap and quickly holding it up to my ear, while adjusting the pitch of that string up or down until the tuning fork and string pitch matched. Then I tuned all the other A strings on the autoharp to match the first one. I tuned the rest of the strings by ear relative to the A strings.

When the instrument was ready to play some real music, the kind of music my grandmother played for me, I'd hand it back to her. Listening to her became my reward for a tuning job well done. She would tear loose—playing and singing one song after another. She may have been only 4' 8" tall, but she became a giant to me when she played.

Just as I tuned Grandma's autoharp so she could make amazing music in my life, God became my Master Tuner. Despite any challenges—and within every celebration—I learned that He knew where He needed me to be, so He could fulfill His will through me. He always met me where I was, then He tuned me at opportune moments until I became something He could use. You could say that I've always been willing to be touched by God, and it honors me when He trusts me with His gifts.

This process continues in my life today. I've had multiple, significant times that shaped my life to bring me to where I am today. Those experiences have been important—and even necessary—for me to fully live out His will.

I would venture that the same is true for you as well. First, we all have *defining moments* that simply happen—that we neither plan nor control. Some are global, like pandemics and wars. We can't avoid them, but they can change the patterns of our lives. Other defining moments happen closer to home, like the birth of a child or death of a loved one. While they don't touch as many people, those who are affected are moved deeply.

Second, we have *threshold moments,* when we stand at a doorway deciding—*Do I do nothing? Do I go straight ahead? Do I turn right or left? Do I turn around and run?* I can always tell threshold moments when I see them, because they force me to make a choice about what to do next. *What should I study at school? Should I take this job? Should I ask Linda to marry me? Should I relocate?* Looking at your own threshold moments, I'm sure you can see how God created those moments to change the trajectory of your life.

I call the third category *ah-ha moments.* When a light turns on in my head and I make a discovery, I know I've just met another ah-ha moment. I've had several of these in my life—when every part of my brain, personality, and intuition come together with God working to connect the dots in such a way that I've often said out loud, *Ah-ha! I know what I need to do now!*

Writing "Rachel's Song" was a defining moment for me. I never set out to write a song on that day—or in that way. "Rachel's Song" just happened, and its creation would take me in a new direction. Along the way, I would face multiple threshold moments, ones that led me to prayer and seeking counsel from my wife, who as I've said, is often my trusted advisor.

And in the process, I encountered many ah-ha moments—where lightbulbs turned on in what had otherwise been a dim room. When the shapes within that room begin to reveal themselves, His work leading up to that moment becomes even more evident.

A Glimpse into My Future

As I mentioned, my travel with AT&T didn't give me much free time to plan or execute my music. I had a client in Nashville, and each week I would fly out on Monday, work all week, then fly back home for the weekend.

But once again, I have a wonderful wife. When I couldn't be thinking about my music, she was. Before one of these trips, Linda had an idea.

"While you're out in Nashville, why don't you get a demo recording made of 'Rachel's Song'?" she suggested. "That would be a wonderful gift for our godchild, Rachel."

Linda's casual suggestion—shrouded in the concept of a gift for this beloved little girl—became a threshold moment. I could have said, "You know, after working such long days, the last thing I want to do is drive around town looking for a recording studio. What I really want to do after a long day on the road is just put my feet up and relax."

Fortunately, however, I stepped towards Linda's idea and said, "What a great idea!"

Little did I know just how great an idea it would be.

In August of 1986, I left work around 7:00 p.m. and headed to downtown Nashville. *Surely*, I thought, *I'll come across a recording studio.* Remember, this was before the internet. After finding more than 200 music studios listed in the phone book Yellow Pages for Nashville, I figured I could throw a rock in any direction and hit one.

With that in mind, I drove to the part of Nashville called Music Square, an area packed with music-related businesses and studios. From my car window, I could see the Country Music Hall of Fame, the historic RCA Victor Studios, BMI headquarters, and several recording studios. However, since it was after 7:00 p.m., most businesses were closed. As we used to say, "They rolled up the sidewalks at five o'clock."

I drove up and down each side street around Music Square several times. I observed the area—with a mixture of residential and businesses, only a few of which were housed in new buildings. Many of the older houses had long since been converted into businesses, which preserved the historical element and space issues that often confront a city's downtown.

Well, this was a bust, I thought to myself. I was about to call it a night. I pulled down Roy Acuff Place, intending to find a way to backtrack to my hotel, when my eye caught a car parked in a gravel parking lot. The building stood out from the others in that area, with an architecture style like a large barn, complete with a water wheel out front. The sign said, "The Music Mill."

Music, I thought. *That sounds promising.*

Pulling into the parking lot, I heard the gravel crunching under my tires. I could see that the lights were on through the glass front door. Peering in from my car in the pre-dusk evening, I glimpsed a man sitting in the lobby behind a big, wooden desk.

On some days, this scene might have made me skeptical. I might have asked myself: *Why is this guy still here past 7:00 p.m., when every other studio is buttoned up? Doesn't he have somewhere else to be?* But God was with me on this evening, and just like when He'd allowed me to play His song, He was allowing me to hear His voice.

Given that all the other studios appear to be closed, I wonder if this is the man I was meant to talk with tonight, I allowed myself to think, surrendering to the idea that God's providence was guiding me. After exiting my car, I walked over and tapped on the glass door. The man rose from the reception desk and began walking to the door, and as he came into sharper focus, I saw that he looked friendly—about my age. He had an easy smile, and he wore glasses and sported a short beard. He unlocked the front door as if he had been waiting just for me.

"Come on in. Can I help you?" he said in a tone that was unusually cheery for someone working in a city that had already begun falling asleep.

"I sure hope so," I replied. "I'm looking for a studio to record a demo of a song I've written." Somehow it always felt odd telling people I'd written the song, since I truly believed

> Somehow it always felt odd telling people I'd written the song, since I truly believed God had written it and given it to me.

God had written it and given it to me. But that was a detail that would have to wait, as surely the man didn't need to know *the whole story* right then.

As I stepped through the doorway, the man grinned and said in his wonderfully familiar Tennessee accent, "Well, I'm George Clinton. And son, if you are looking for a studio, you're in one."

As I looked around the room, I realized this was no ordinary place. The walls of the lobby were covered with large photos of famous groups like Alabama, Glen Campbell, and The Forester Sisters—and several groupings of framed gold and platinum records. Turns out that I had happened upon one of Nashville's top recording studios. And George, I later learned, was one of the most respected and loved recording engineers in Nashville, as well as a true Southern gentleman.

Today, that iconic building that I stumbled into after driving the city streets of Nashville serves as the headquarters for the Nashville Songwriters Association International (NSAI). The waterwheel still sits out front.

I learned that Harold Shedd, a well-known music producer for many award-winning groups, owned the Music Mill. But George Clinton, the man I had the pleasure to meet when I stepped through that front door, seemed like one of those rare people who felt like an instant friend. We hit it right off.

"I have to be honest, George," I told him. "I've never been in a recording studio before." Thinking back, I'm sure he already knew that from the questions I immediately started asking him.

George graciously listened to each question, then he made me an offer I couldn't decline.

"How'd you like to tour the place?"

"Really? I would love that," I told him with the excitement of a kid.

"All right then!" He slapped his hands together. "Let me show you our Studio A, which just happens to be vacant right now."

As we walked into the main Studio A, I couldn't believe how big it was. I surmised that it could easily accommodate a full orchestra. A large, black, concert grand piano sat in one corner. Around the perimeter of the large room were smaller, glass-enclosed rooms. George explained how they used these small rooms as isolation rooms for singers and drummers. A bit awestruck, I followed my new friend.

Finally, he opened a very thick, heavy door.

"You feel how heavy that is? That's because it's soundproof," George explained.

We stepped into what George told me was the control room. It looked like what I'd expect to see at NASA! I mean, with all the dials, switches, and gauges, it looked like you could land rockets on the moon with the electronics in this room. The scene would have been a little boy's dream, and even at my age—and especially with my lifelong love of music—it was a bit like being invited to witness an important slice of history. It wasn't just a room to me, but the place where dreams had been made.

My awe continued.

Pointing to an eight-foot-wide console, George told me, "This can accommodate thirty-two simultaneous recording channels." Turning to an empty chair, he continued, "That's where the recording engineer sits. He uses two analog tape-recording machines. You probably already have a tape recorder. Think of this like a giant version of that. We record on two-inch wide tapes running at 30 inches per second. That's why music recorded at a studio like this sounds crystal clear. What do you think?" he asked.

"I think it's amazing," I responded, telling him that while I worked with high-end computers, this was unlike anything I'd imagined. "So let me ask you this, George," I said gearing up for *the big question*: "How much does it cost to rent a studio like this?"

"$125 an hour, plus engineer."

"Wow, that's a lot of money," I told him.

Remember, this was 1986. In 2021 dollars, that would be nearly $300.

"I hear you," George said. "Think of this as the Cadillac of music studios. But don't worry. The owner, Harold, has another studio across the street called Studio 803. It used to be called Wild Tracks. It's a great studio, especially if this is your first recording. That one is more like a Chevrolet, and there is nothing wrong with that! Besides, it's only $15 an hour, plus engineer."

"Now you're talking!" I told him enthusiastically. "That's more my speed."

After thinking a moment, I had one more question for George. "Do you know a good piano player who could help me make a demo? I've written this song called 'Rachel's Song,' and I think it's something special."

"A session piano player," he said half to himself. Then he nodded his head. "You know, I think I've got the right person for you. We attend the same church. His name's Gary Prim. He's quite a talented session musician. Let me take you back up front, and I'll get his phone number for you."

Once we got to George's desk, he spun his Rolodex until he found what he was looking for. He wrote down Gary's name and number on a slip of paper and handed it to me.

"The more I think about it, the more I'm convinced that Gary is your man. Give him a call. I'm sure he will be happy to help you," George told me.

Immediately after I left the studio, I headed straight to my hotel and called Gary on the hotel phone. (This is before cell phones were common.) But instead of reaching him, I got his answering machine.

"Hello, this is Gary. Leave me a message, and I will call you back," a friendly voice told me before a beep.

On my message, I told him who I was and that he'd come highly recommended by George Clinton. Then I left him my number at the hotel with a request that he call me as soon as he could.

After I hung up, I really wanted to call Linda to tell her all about my visit with George at the studio. But I thought, *I better not get on the phone now. I don't want to miss Gary if he calls me back!* (This was also before call waiting was built into nearly every phone line's service plan.) Sitting in my quiet hotel room, my mind drifted in nervous anticipation. *Will Gary be willing to do this for me? I wonder how much it would cost. What would a demo recording really sound like?*

I didn't have long to wait. After about thirty minutes, the phone rang; it was Gary. His very friendly voice asked how he could help me.

"Well, I have written this simple instrumental piece called 'Rachel's Song,' and I would like to get a good demo recording of it on piano. Is that something you could do for me?"

"Why sure!" he said with genuine enthusiasm. You know how they say you can hear a smile in someone's voice over the phone? Well, I heard Gary's smile, and I instantly knew that I would really enjoy working with him. "Just send me a lead sheet and a recording of you playing it, and I will be happy to do that."

"I would love to do that, Gary. But one thing: *what's a lead sheet?*" I asked, candidly showing my lack of knowledge about the music industry.

"Oh, that's just the melody written out along with the chords," Gary explained.

"Oh, good! Because I do have that. I just didn't know what to call it," I said, feeling relieved that it wasn't something complicated that I'd need to create.

"Just send it over, give me a couple of weeks, and we'll be ready to record," he said.

"That works just fine for me," I told him as my excitement grew. "I'll be back here in Nashville in a couple of weeks working on a project. The timing works out great. One more question, Gary. How much do you charge for the demo recording?"

"Just $25," he said.

"Wow! I was expecting a lot more than that," I replied.

"Demo rates for studio musicians are a lot less than full-scale rates for recording albums," he explained.

After taking down Gary's mailing address, I thanked him for his help and said goodbye.

When I hung up the phone, I had no idea that neither Gary's life nor mine would ever be the same after that. Writing "Rachel's Song" had already created a *defining moment.* Taking Linda's advice to get a demo recording made while I worked in Nashville was a *threshold moment.* And that night, finding George who led me to Gary, would soon take me to more than one *ah-ha moment!*

CHAPTER TWO

IS THAT MY SONG?

"Thank you for producing the beautiful music of your heart.
Your music really helps me through the many storms in my life."
~William

As soon as I got back home to Winston-Salem, I made a cassette recording of me playing "Rachel's Song" and sent it along with a copy of the lead sheet to Gary.

Before I took my next trip to Nashville, Gary let me know that he had already booked studio time! We would record "Rachel's Song" at 6:00 p.m. on Friday evening, August 22, 1986—at the small studio located in a house across the street from the Music Mill. This was the place that George Clinton had told me about, simply called Studio 803.

Studio 803

Do you remember that feeling of being a child on Christmas Eve? That's how I felt the whole day of August 22. I brimmed with anticipation, and excitement pulsed through me.

It was a Friday afternoon and it was near the appointed time. I arrived a few minutes before six and parked in the driveway immediately behind the house studio. From the outside, it just looked like a simple, small house. It didn't even have a sign out front, just the house number: 803.

Little did I know at the time that I would never forget that address.

I sprang up the stairs to the front porch and tried not to knock as hard as my excitement was making me feel. As the door swung open, a friendly young fellow appeared and quickly introduced himself as "Three-Dollar," the recording engineer.

"You can just call me Three for short," he said. I hoped that's how much he'd be charging me for the hour. But before I even had a chance to ask, he explained how he'd acquired that unusual nickname.

"I'm from Alabama originally. I started in music by setting up sound equipment for many different bands. Most musicians don't have much money, but each time I'd set up their sound equipment, they'd give me $3. After a while," he laughed, "that became my new name. Three-Dollar."

Another detail I'd never forget.

Once inside, I looked around. I could see that this studio had originally been a small, two-bedroom, one-bathroom house. The left side of the house had been converted into the recording studio. What had been the front bedroom was now the main studio, with an old Yamaha baby grand piano. Behind that room toward the back was the control room, which was separated from the studio by a soundproof glass window and heavy soundproof door. The control room held all the recording equipment, which consisted of a 24-track console and a 2-track quarter-inch tape recorder—as in the other studio, just a bit older. I learned that the room holding the Yamaha baby grand piano did triple duty as it was also used to record drums and vocals. All the walls were lined with burlap and other material for absorbing sound.

Before I left, I learned that the Yamaha in this very studio had been the first grand piano ever shipped to Nashville by Yamaha. I could picture some of the famous, great Nashville musicians back in the day, like Floyd Cramer and Hargus "Pig" Robbins, playing and recording music on this historic piano over the years. The thoughts that "Rachel's Song" might make its own history using this treasure from the past made my heart soar!

> **The thoughts that "Rachel's Song" might make its own history using this treasure from the past made my heart soar!**

Gary Prim Adds His Special Touch

At 6:00 p.m. sharp, Gary Prim swept through the door. He was about my height, trim, casually dressed, and wearing a baseball cap—just as I had pictured him in my mind. Like with George Clinton, I felt a special connection to Gary instantly, and we hit it off before the door closed behind him. Gary was friendly, soft-spoken, and easy to get to know. He carried his Yamaha DX-7 synthesizer keyboard under his arm. After we talked for a few minutes, he began setting up his equipment.

"Hey, Three-Dollar," he said, as if he were talking to an old friend. "Life been good to you?"

"It's great. Life treats me the same way I treat it," Three-Dollar replied as the two of them shook hands.

The studio did not have a stand for the keyboard, so Three helped Gary set it up on a simple wooden crate, like the ones used to store and sell apples. As I watched Gary and Three get everything set, I noted how efficiently they worked. No sir, they didn't waste any time getting ready to record. I thought to myself: *They really know what they are doing. My only job here is to stay out of their way. Boy, is this ever an education!*

Gary sat down at the piano and began playing a little, warming up his fingers and familiarizing himself with the feel of the keys and sound of this piano. At the same time, Three sat at the console, checking sound level and sound quality. Then he connected two microphones to record the piano in stereo on tracks 5 and 6 of the 2-inch 24-track master tape.

I stayed back in the control room with the engineer. On the outside, I hoped I looked like the mature, calm businessman I was by day. But on the inside, I was so excited I couldn't stand it.

Three communicated to Gary from the control room through a small speaker mounted in the studio. He'd push a button to speak, and Gary could hear him. As soon as Three and Gary both indicated they were ready to go, Three pushed the record button on the 2-inch tape recorder, held down the talk button, and told Gary, "We're rollin.'"

I could see Gary through the soundproof window—and clearly hear him and the piano through the monitor speakers in the control room. Gary started to play his arrangement of "Rachel's Song."

Prior to a few weeks before this evening, I'd never stepped foot in a recording studio. And now I was not only in a studio, but I got to watch years of my life interpreted, compressed, and recorded in a few minutes. Hours earlier, I had no idea what to expect.

Whatever I'd envisioned fell short of the grand experience unfolding before my eyes and ears. It's not that I was impressed by the technology—or the fact that I was in Nashville. I worked in

Whatever I'd envisioned fell short of the grand experience unfolding before my eyes and ears.

technology and had spent weeks at a time in this city. No, what left me awestruck was hearing a professional musician playing my own "Rachel's Song." Despite knowing each melody note before Gary played it, the beauty of the sound stuck somewhere between my ears and my throat, and emotions swept over me. Simply put, I could not believe my ears.

Gary got several measures into the song, then stopped and played three or four side-by-side, discordant notes—like C, D, and E a couple of times—as a signal to Three to stop recording. Imagine hearing someone playing "Moonlight Sonata" by Beethoven, then having a herd of cats run across the keyboard. That's what the unmistakable "stop recording" signal sounded like.

The monitor speaker crackled, and Gary said, "Hey Three, could we roll back the tape, and let me do that one more time?"

I quickly learned that Gary was quite a perfectionist with his playing and recording, something I greatly appreciated.

Three rewound the 2-inch tape to the beginning, pushed record, and spoke back to Gary again, "We're rollin."

This time, Gary got all the way through the song, playing the verse and chorus three times—with the first two times in the key of C, and then a sudden, dramatic key change up a half-step to the key of D flat on the third time through. The key change caught me by surprise and raised the impact of the music to another level. *I can't believe what I am hearing*, I thought to myself.

When Gary stopped playing, I figured we were done. But he wasn't.

"Three, I want to add a richer tone. Let me run through it again with the DX-7," Gary said, referring to his electric keyboard. "That'll play off the quiet opening and first verse."

Three rolled back the 2-inch tape to the beginning, switched the recording channels to 7 and 8, and switched the input to come from the

DX-7. Then Three played the piano music back so Gary could hear it playing on channels 5 and 6 in his headphones, while also hearing the live tone from his electric piano as he played along in real time. Gary's precision was flawless—how he matched the play of the electric piano exactly, note for note, with what he heard from the grand piano in his headset. I learned that in recording lingo, they call this *doubling*. Gary did this doubling of the piano to the end of the song. As a result, the sound became much fuller and richer.

It just keeps getting better, I thought to myself. But much to my delight, he wasn't finished yet. Gary wanted to add some musical punch in select places, so he included horns. Gary switched the DX-7 to the horns sound, and Three readied the 2-inch tape to record the horns on tracks 9 and 10. Then he played back the piano and electric piano on their respective tracks. Three rolled the tape, and Gary masterfully played the horns sound in exactly the right places. *Amazing!*

"You get that, Three?" Gary asked through the studio mic.

"Got it," Three confirmed.

"Great," Gary smiled. "Let's go back again. I want to add two tracks of strings."

Gary later told me that strings would fill out the sound—giving it some bottom (low notes) and top (high notes). Once again, Three set up his console, assigning the string tracks to record on tracks 13 and 14. Gary switched the DX-7 to his choice strings sound. Three set the piano, electric piano, and horns tracks to "play" mode, so that we, and Gary, could hear them while he added the strings sound. Three rolled tape, and Gary started playing the strings sound. Wow! I'm not sure what look I had on my face when I heard "Rachel's Song" played with all the tracks added, but there's a good chance that my mouth stayed popped open.

Is This My "Rachel's Song"?

Hearing Gary play "Rachel's Song" for the first time filled me with so many simultaneous emotions of amazement and awe. And disbelief.

Could this possibly be the simple song I had written? Is it possible that God used my fingers to create something so beautiful? I asked myself.

I'd always felt as if God had given me this song. Even when I called it *my* song, it was with full reverence of *His* gift. And now, years later, I stood in a home converted into a music studio—witnessing the new birth of my song, one that would change my life—and, as it would turn out, the life of Gary Prim as well.

After laying the final track, Gary removed his headphones and joined us in the control room, where we listened to the whole mixture of sounds. Gary saw a couple of places he wanted to improve. He and Three Dollar re-worked just those precise parts, without disturbing anything before or after them. They called this process "punching in," which is graphically what it looked like to me.

Gary returned to the room with the Yamaha. At the precise moments, Gary would nod his head through the glass window, and Three Dollar would punch the record button simultaneously. Gary would keep playing and re-record a particular passage—until he nodded, signaling Three to punch the record button again to turn it off.

The whole process fascinated me—both as a musician, and someone who had worked close to technology throughout my career. More importantly, I just couldn't believe the sound I was hearing. I never believed that any music that I could have written could sound *that good*. I was on cloud nine. I only wished Linda was there watching this all unfold with me, especially since she had been the one prompting me to record!

Within an hour—and for only $25—Gary finished recording. I must have thanked him at least twenty times. I wrote Gary a modest check for our agreed-upon fee.

(Just so you don't think I was a cheapskate and didn't pay Gary enough, I was glad to pay him more a few weeks later when I realized that the music he had recorded was destined to be *much more* than just a demo recording. I ended up paying Gary full union scale for the recording session.)

As Gary wrapped up his work, he thanked me for the opportunity to play my music. Little did either of us know that our relationship and the music we created that evening would grow exponentially over the coming years.

Three Adds His Special Touches

Once Gary left the studio, Three started to work his own brand of creativity.

"So now I need to get the right mix of all these tracks to create a stereo master tape for you," he said as I started to understand more of the music industry lingo. Three spent about thirty minutes balancing the sound of the piano and other instruments, until he got it exactly right. Three's wonderworking was called "mixing," which proved he had the phenomenal ear and talent of a professional recording engineer.

Once Three felt satisfied with the mix, he smiled and nodded his head up and down in approval of what he heard.

"I'm going to send you home with a master tape," he told me—while his fingers hit buttons, turned dials, and slid faders (volume controls that slide up and down), with the same speed my fingers could hit piano keys. "From this tape, you'll be able to make either records or cassettes, whichever you like."

(In 1986, CDs weren't in the picture quite yet. The master tape was a quarter inch, reel to reel, two-track tape recorded at 15 inches per second [ips].)

Three also made me a quarter inch master tape at 7 ½ ips that I could play at home on my Sony reel-to-reel tape recorder. Finally, he ran off four cassette tape copies of the recording, so that I could play one on my rental car cassette player.

I couldn't write Three the $30 check for studio time and another $25 for his engineering services fast enough. Added to the $25 I'd paid Gary, my total cost was $80 for the finished recording. *Well worth it for this tape, and the experience of watching it get made!* I thought as my hands shook a bit, trying to hold the pen to the paper. I was on a "music high," which is like the runner's high athletes feel when the adrenaline flows through their bodies from strenuous exercise.

> **I was on a "music high," which is like the runner's high athletes feel when the adrenaline flows through their bodies from strenuous exercise.**

With my new treasures in hand, I thanked Three and left Studio 803 with my head and heart full of music.

As I walked to my car, I realized that my handwritten tune had transformed from a mere slip of paper to a masterful, professionally recorded demo of "Rachel's Song" in less than two hours. Again, I was awestruck. With the notes still dancing in my head, I probably wouldn't have noticed if a thunderstorm had broken out, dumping sheets of rain on me (fortunately, it hadn't!).

By the way, this is the same unedited and identical recording that is still on my "Rachel's Song" album. Talk about *getting it right the first time*. "Rachel's Song" never needed to be re-recorded or edited, thanks to the talents of Gary and Three. Boy, did I feel grateful to George Clinton for pointing me to Studio 803!

Before you continue reading, I would like to invite you to join me back in the studio on that August evening in 1986. The closest way you can experience those moments is to play "Rachel's Song." If you don't already own your own copy of "Rachel's Song," you can go to your favorite online music source (i.e. iTunes, Apple Music, or Amazon) and search for "Rachel's Song Gary Prim." You can also stream on your favorite streaming music sources (i.e. Spotify, iHeart Radio, Pandora). Or you can use this QR code to take you directly to the Combs Music website at CombsMusic.com. Just point your mobile phone camera at the code.

Once you hit play, close your eyes. Picture the control room—with me and the engineer. See Gary with his skilled fingers artfully playing the Yamaha baby grand piano. Replay that recording session in your imagination. Let the music flow over you just like it did for me that hot summer night in Nashville. You will be blessed.

Alone with "Rachel's Song"

When I flew into Nashville for this trip, I had intentionally rented a car with a cassette player in anticipation of getting the recording done. As I got into the driver's seat of my rental car, I turned on the ignition, and before I even put the car into gear, I pushed one of the cassette tapes into the opening of the tape player and turned up the volume. I sat in the parking lot and listened to "Rachel's Song," experiencing it as if it were the first time God had gifted me with the tune.

Driving back to the hotel, I felt on top of the world. I was on such an emotional high that I was oblivious to any traffic I encountered on my way back to my hotel! The experience—and outcome—had been as grand as the piano my song was played on; I was filled with gratitude that the pieces had fallen into place so seamlessly.

Needless to say, the bright lights of Nashville streaming through my windshield were the furthest thing from my mind. Instead, my mind wandered with the music.

Not quite six years earlier, I had sat in my basement back in North Carolina—in front of my old Knabe baby grand piano—when my fingers explored the keyboard, and the first notes of "Rachel's Song" sounded. The tune that emerged then served as a defining moment in my life. My wife's suggestion to record "Rachel's Song" became a threshold moment, one that I eagerly accepted. But inside my rental car driving along the interstate that evening in Nashville, I became overwhelmed. Listening to "Rachel's Song" over and over again, I finally said to myself, "This is it! This is it! THIS IS IT!"

Of course, I had no idea what "it" would turn out to be, but I knew an ah-ha moment when it appeared to me. And in that instant, I knew in my heart that "Rachel's Song" would change my life.

Not every journey we embark on happens on tidy, paved, straight paths. The same holds true for the complicated network of interstate highways in Nashville, especially around the I-40, I-24, and I-65 exits. Unless you really pay attention, you'll likely find yourself in the wrong lane and needing to make another loop around to catch your exit. Which is exactly what happened to me. I found myself so absorbed in the music, I missed my exit. Not until I passed the same billboards a few times did this fact dawn on me! Actually, I think I circled Nashville at least two or three times.

Whenever we are at the brink of a discovery, it's common that our minds and physical bodies seem separate from each other. I navigated and drove on autopilot, apparently doing a better job on the driving part than the navigating part. But my mind drifted miles away, as if it were stretching out to connect some dots that seemed just out of reach.

Eventually, my body and mind got back in sync, and I made my way to my hotel—bursting with excitement to share my music with Linda.

But that would have to wait.

CHAPTER THREE

I Don't Know What *It* Is, But I Know There's a Plan

"I have never been so touched. In a world full of stress and daily battles, it is nice to have something that can put everything back into perspective."
~Jo

I couldn't wait to call my wife. I think I literally ran to the phone in my hotel room to call her the moment I entered my room. But I'd have to wait to share the music with her. The only phone I had was attached by a cord to my hotel room's wall. And the only cassette player I had was inside my rental car. I had nothing with which to play the recording in the hotel room.

So instead of "showing" her my music, I told her about my experience in such detail that I hoped she could picture—and *hear*—everything herself.

"Oh, Linda, I wish you could have been here with me. It took my breath away watching and listening to 'Rachel's Song' come off the page and onto the piano through Gary Prim's fingers! I would give anything to play this demo for you right now, so you could hear it for yourself," I told her in between gulps of excitement.

My, how times have changed. Today, I would connect Linda "live" with me in the studio, using Facetime or any number of apps. And I would walk out of the studio with a thumb drive of the recording in my pocket and a link via email or text message, so I could send it anywhere in the world.

"And Linda, Gary didn't just play it on the piano; he added other instruments too, using his synthesizer," I shared as I relived my own excitement. "Gary decided to add some rich tones to the piano, so he did another track with his electric piano. Then, he still wasn't done. He added tracks with horns and strings, too. And let me tell you about Three…." I gushed on.

Linda tried to picture the studio and imagine hearing the music from my description alone. But she didn't have to imagine my enthusiasm. She could feel it through the more than 400 miles of phone line that connected us. From my voice, she sensed that this moment was a life-changer.

From my voice, she sensed that this moment was a life-changer.

Rachel's Song Goes Live—at Circuit City

After I talked with Linda, I had too much excitement to stay in my hotel room. I felt desperate to share this new music with someone, even a stranger. The feeling was like when I'd asked Linda to marry me, and she said yes. I just wanted to tell the world!

I drove away with the thought of sharing "Rachel's Song" with the world, when I spotted a Circuit City. As an electronics store, I knew they would have a big display of speakers and stereos. In no time, I found a salesclerk.

"I wonder if you would do something for me," I started off saying.

Before long, the clerk acquiesced to my request, putting my cassette tape into a high-end stereo system, hooked up to their high-quality speakers.

"Oh," I added. "Can you really turn it up?"

The instant the sweet sounds of "Rachel's Song" rang out across the large store, customers and employees alike stopped in their tracks to listen, just as I had expected they would. I saw firsthand, and for the first time, the effect that the newly recorded "Rachel's Song" had on others.

At that moment, I whispered to myself once again, *This is it! This is it!* While I still didn't know what it referred to, I knew something with certainty: "Rachel's Song" held the power to touch others in a deep and profound way. Something seemed to be shifting the trajectory of that song. Each time the music was played, it was as if the launching pad were being prepared—with the rocket powered for liftoff.

What will happen next? I couldn't help but wonder. *Where will this song travel next?*

"Do You Mind If I Play Some Music?"

My AT&T team and I worked through that weekend on a computer system cutover to the new manufacturing software for the Nashville factory. We had toiled on this project for months. Each time my team and I got in my car to get lunch or dinner, I popped "Rachel's Song" into the cassette player.

This response, and many more like it, confirmed that I held something special.

"You're saying you wrote this?" a colleague asked with a blend of skepticism and admiration.

"Yes, I did. This is the song I've been telling you about," I confirmed.

"It's just..." he paused as he searched for the right words. "It's just so beautiful, like it's both happy and sad at the same time, like our memories."

This response, and many more like it, confirmed that I held something special.

"If you can create something like this," one told me, "What the heck are you doing working with AT&T?"

"Seriously, you've got to get this out there," another told me.

This encouragement motivated me. I knew I needed to do something to make "Rachel's Song" widely available.

Making the demo tape took me over the *threshold*, but the specifics of the *ah-ha* were still beyond my immediate grasp.

"Linda, You Are Not Going to Believe Your Ears!"

I couldn't wait to complete our work on the computer system, so I could fly home to see Linda. But let me be honest. What I most anticipated on return from this trip wasn't seeing her beautiful, smiling face again—but rather sharing "Rachel's Song" with her for the first time.

After walking into the house, I dropped my suitcase and gave my wife a big hug and kiss. Knowing my excitement, Linda did not protest when I clutched her hand and made a beeline to our stereo system. I placed the cassette in the player, hit play, and sat with her—anticipating what would come next.

As we held hands listening to the recording of "Rachels' Song" for the first time together, something shifted in me. Normally, I didn't (and still don't) easily express my emotions openly. Either by temperament or habit, I'd usually keep them inside. As I looked over at Linda, I saw tears of joy flowing freely down her cheeks as she squeezed my hand. That's when I felt my own eyes fill with tears. I flashed back to the same experience I'd had while playing "Rachel's Song" at Rachel's christening. Something about this song touched me—still.

Who else could it touch? I barely allowed myself to wonder this, as I relished the moment. But clearly, this rocket was powered—capable of liftoff.

Linda had heard me play this song many times on the piano—for more than five years, to be exact. But hearing it with the richness of the additional instruments Gary had added left her speechless. I'll bet we rewound and played "Rachel's Song" at least a dozen times before we got up.

Linda's emotions and encouragement overwhelmed me. I was honored to witness her response—and floored by the intensity emanating from this song. I said, "I know this is *it*, but now what? What do we do with this beautiful song?

Where Do We Go from Here?

Neither Linda nor I had an immediate answer to that question. But without saying anything, we both trusted an answer would come.

My faith had never allowed me to place my future in the hands of mere coincidences. Instead, I learned about the concept written about by author Squire Rushnell, called a "Godwink." A Godwink is like a coincidence, but it is personal and unmistakable. It may seem like random things falling into place. But a Godwink is God-directed, and it's like God giving you a wink to say, "There you go! You are on the right path. What just happened was not an accident." By my estimation, throughout my life, I'd say God has given me these "there you go" moments hundreds, if not thousands of times.

> **A Godwink is like a coincidence, but it is personal and unmistakable.**

I've often heard that old saying, "God doesn't give us more than we can handle." Instead, I believe that God helps us handle what we are given. How does God do that? He puts us in situations where we need to trust Him, and He brings people and circumstances into our lives to help guide us along the path. He doesn't twist our arms or force us to do anything against our will. But if we have faith, He does patiently lead us to where He wants us.

I can't count the number of times in my life when I had planned to do one thing, but God intervened through events and other people to redirect my thoughts and actions. I don't call that luck. I call that being blessed, and I do consider myself extremely blessed. Every event in my life—and I mean the times when joy took me to the mountaintop, and sorrow brought me to the valley—God used all those times. Those times led me to this moment, when Linda and I sat in our living room—holding hands, feeling blessed and grateful, and listening to the beautiful music of "Rachel's Song."

This is it! kept echoing in my head, but I still didn't know how to define it or what to do with it.

Then it dawned on me. I didn't have to know. God knew. He had taken me from the mountains of East Tennessee and provided a way for me to go to college through the kindness and initiative of lifelong friends (the details of which I will share later). He also used another man, Stan Johnson, to introduce me to computers, which prompted me to study something I loved. Then Stan helped me find a great job with Western Electric. God had put various opportunities in my life to help me become an entrepreneur and run a business.

And then, he had placed "Rachel's Song" in my heart, brought me to Nashville, directed my path to George Clinton—who, in turn, pointed me to Gary Prim.

I figured I was okay not knowing what *it* meant or what to do with *it*. God would show me at the right time.

Quite honestly, God surprised me with how quickly that time would come.

CHAPTER FOUR

THE PLAN FOR THE MUSIC BEGINS BEING REVEALED

*"I will never tire of your music. Please promise me one thing.
You will never stop composing music."*
~FRANK

In early September of 1986, I had lunch with my friend, Bob McHone.
When I told Bob about my trip to Nashville and recording "Rachel's
Song," he became intrigued. He could easily see how excited and
energized I was.

"I'd love to hear it, Dave," Bob reciprocated with enthusiasm.

"And I would love for you to hear it, too," I answered with excitement.
"You have a cassette player in your office, right?"

"Oh, you know I do," Bob answered.

"How about we head to your office, and I play it for you there?"

Bob nodded. "Let's do that."

Soon after lunch, we headed to Bob's small, organized office. I handed
him the cassette copy of "Rachel's Song" to play. We sat down to listen.

As the song began to fill the room, Bob leaned forward in his chair,
closer to the stereo. He closed his eyes and listened intently as if to not
miss a single note. Bob was an experienced broadcaster with an excellent
ear for good music. He also had a very expressive face, which gave
away his emotions. When the music reached a crescendo and instantly
changed keys, Bob opened his eyes, looked at me, and softly said, "Oh
my!" With tears running down his cheeks, he waited until the song
finished before speaking, with emotion cracking in his voice. "Beautiful!
Beautiful! That's a standard."

Then he added, "You must let me play this song on my radio program."

I had almost forgotten that Bob hosted a weekly, three-hour, big band
jazz music program on our local easy-listening radio station, WKLM-
FM 94.5. I agreed for him to play my song. But he needed a high-quality
version of the music. And the only copy I had was my quarter-inch, reel-
to-reel master tape.

The next day, I took Bob the master recording, still a bit nervous about letting it out of my hands. But I trusted that Bob would not let anything happen to it.

He took it to the radio station, where they made a high-quality copy of the recording on a Fidelipac master tape cartridge (*cart*, as they called it) that could be played on the radio station equipment.

Later that day, Bob returned my master tape.

As he handed the tape to me, he said, "Here you go, Dave. Now don't forget to listen to the program tomorrow. I can't wait for my listeners to hear 'Rachel's Song'!"

"Rachel's Song" Hits the Airwaves

The next morning, Saturday, Linda and I indeed did tune in to listen. We sat at home holding hands, as our stereo FM radio was tuned to 94.5 FM. Bob's program began with his wonderful, smooth radio voice—which was instantly recognizable and distinct. I loved to tell him that he was the Paul Harvey of Winston-Salem!

Bob began by announcing a slight change to his normal music program. He introduced the song by saying, "I'm going to deviate from my normal big band and jazz music this morning and play a song recently recorded in Nashville by my good friend, Dave Combs of Winston-Salem. I trust you'll be as moved by it as I was when I first heard it a few days ago. It's called 'Rachel's Song.'"

Linda and I felt goosebumps shoot up and down our arms as the first notes began to play. We were thrilled beyond measure to hear "Rachel's Song" playing on the radio for the first time—and so grateful to Bob for giving the song such a special introduction and airing.

But we weren't ready for what would happen next. The station manager at WKLM called.

"Dave, I have never experienced this phenomenon in my entire radio career," he said, sounding a little breathless. "As soon as 'Rachel's Song' started to play, the phone lines all lit up at the same time and stayed that

> **Linda and I looked at one another with our mouths open.** *Where can they get a copy of it? What a great question.*

way constantly. They all had the same questions. 'What was that song you just played by that guy from Winston-Salem?', 'Will you please play it again?', and 'Where can I get a copy of it?'"

Linda and I looked at one another with our mouths open. *Where can they get a copy of it? What a great question.*

"Rachel's Song" Touches a Broader Audience and Fan Mail Begins

Linda and I were both so excited that people wanted copies of "Rachel's Song" that I sprang into immediate action.

A couple of days later, I purchased a double-deck cassette machine, capable of playing one cassette on one side while duplicating it on the other cassette. Creating copies of "Rachel's Song" became my "second job." When I wasn't working or sleeping, I made cassette copies at home, one by one. I sold copies of the song for the mere cost of a blank cassette. Everybody we knew wanted a copy, and the demand quickly outran my capability to duplicate cassettes in real time.

Everywhere I went—work, church, and with neighbors or friends—I took every opportunity to play the "Rachel's Song" recording to anybody who would listen. Since everyone who heard the song wanted a copy, I sold hundreds of cassettes. Once I added in the time it took me to make each cassette, of course I lost money. But I wanted to share "Rachel's Song" with the world, and by starting with the people I knew, I began putting a small dent in reaching at least North Carolina.

At the same time, "Rachel's Song" got picked up by more local radio stations. Then it picked up momentum across the whole country! That's when I received something that I didn't remember getting during all my years with AT&T—fan mail!

At first, I got a few letters. Then hundreds poured in. Then thousands!

This was the first of many fan letters.

"Waiting in my car during the Christmas rush, your 'Rachel's Song' came on over my local radio station. The simplicity and beauty of your music made a memorable and pleasant occasion out of the traffic jam!" ~Dixon

One special letter came from a dear woman whose daughter, Rachel, had died of a brain tumor. She told me that the soothing melody brought back wonderful memories of her own Rachel, every time

At first, I got a few letters. Then hundreds poured in. Then thousands!

she heard it. Another note came with a photo of a beaming girl with autism, hugging the tape to her chest with tears running down her cheeks.

"Your music reached her," the note read.

Doctors and nurses wrote to tell me that my music had calmed their patients. Several brides told me that they had chosen it for their weddings. Teachers confided that my music settled down their students. Artists told me that they listened to my music to increase their creativity. Ministers said that they played my music when they wrote their sermons. Recovering alcoholics said my music helped enable their quest to maintain sobriety.

"Rachel's Song" Gets the 45-rpm Treatment

Realizing that cassette tapes were not the quality recordings that radio stations needed, I had to find a better way to reach more radio stations' program directors, the folks who decided what music got played. I knew if I could get a high-quality copy of "Rachel's Song" to program directors at easy-listening radio stations nationwide, the song would spread even faster. Cassette tapes wouldn't do it. I needed a 45-rpm vinyl record.

So, on one of my next business trips to Nashville, I went to see the folks at United Record Pressing. They told me exactly what I needed to do to get 45-rpm vinyl records made. First, I needed to provide them with what they called *metal stampers* to literally press the vinyl records. To get my metal stampers, they recommended that I use Master-

Mix Studios—located at 1921 Division Street in Nashville, owned by mastering engineer Hank Williams (no relation to the famous singer). I made an appointment with Hank to coincide with my next business trip to Nashville. Once I arrived, I handed him my master tape and watched with fascination as he cut the music onto a lacquer disc using a diamond stylus. Then, he metal-plated the disc to make a metal stamper. Master-Mix sent the stampers to United Record Pressing directly. Lastly, I provided United Record Pressing with the graphics layout for the label.

I ordered 400 records as a pilot test of sorts. Since I only had one song, I had them put "Rachel's Song" on both sides of the record. In music business lingo, they called it a *double-A single* since it did not have a B-side.

Then I waited for what felt like a lifetime to get my shipment of 45-rpm records. The days passed slowly, reminding me of the saying, "a watched pot never boils."

While the wait seemed interminable, in about three weeks, the heavy box made it to my doorstep. With fingers twitching in excitement, I opened the box and looked at the stack of 45-rpm treasures secured within! Finally, I had a quality product I could use to promote "Rachel's Song" to an even wider audience.

"Rachel's Song" Appears in Its First Record Shop

I decided to start local in my efforts to get the new products distributed, so I approached our locally owned record store, Reznick's Records at Thruway Shopping Center. Normally when I would pop inside, I was looking to buy some music. But this time, I wanted to share something of my own.

"Hi, Mrs. Reznick," I said, entering her shop. "How are you today?"

"Hello, Dave," she smiled. "I'm doing great. What can I help you find today?"

"Well, actually, I am here to play you a song of my own," I smiled back. "Care to give it a listen?"

After she heard it, she was eager to sell the 45-rpm recording.

The Reznick family will always hold a special place in my heart, as their store was the first retail establishment to sell my music.

"I just love 'Rachel's Song,'" Mrs. Reznick told me when I came in a short time later. "But do you know what's even better? My customers love it too. And once they hear it, they buy a copy!"

Muzak Meets "Rachel's Song"

I continued to contact as many easy-listening stations and music-programming distribution companies as I could find in my spare time. I sent them the "Rachel's Song" 45 record, and virtually all of them started programming "Rachel's Song" for airplay. Since the song fell into the easy-listening category, one of those music-programming companies was Muzak (now Mood Media). They were known for providing background music, sometimes called "elevator music." I called the Muzak headquarters in Seattle, Washington, sent them "Rachel's Song," and they became one of the first companies that programmed my music. I quickly learned that many companies—such as airlines, hotels, grocery store chains, and restaurants—used the Muzak music service.

It always gave me a special thrill when I entered businesses across the country and heard my music being played! One day, I was walking through the Atlanta airport, and as I entered the terminal that led to my gate, playing all through that terminal was "Rachel's Song!" Another time, I was in a grocery store when I heard my music playing. Those experiences never failed to bring me a smile—and the reassurance that I was *doing the right thing* with my music.

How Far Can "Rachel's Song" Go?

I wanted to apply the principle of duplication to "Rachel's Song." *If one radio station generated X number of sales, what would happen if I had five, ten, a hundred, or a thousand radio stations playing it?*

Since "Rachel's Song" generated an overwhelming response at WKLM-FM, I started thinking exponentially—back to the mathematical concept in business about compound interest. Compounding interest intrigued me in college as a math major. After listening to an insurance salesman trying to sell me whole life insurance while I was still in school, I became intrigued by his guarantee of what sounded to me like an unbelievable return on my investment. So, I did what all math students with access to a computer would do: I plotted the growth rate of the return using a computer program. I found that the insurance salesman was right. If I invested around $10,000 a year over twenty-five years at a 10 percent return, I would have a million dollars! That really made an impression on me. And it turned out the principles of replication, duplication, and compound interest had direct application to my growing music business.

With that in mind, I got my hands on a copy of a publication called Radio and Records, which listed all radio stations in the country by format. I wasted no time in calling easy-listening stations in all the major markets in the United States. In the process, I learned something critical: many of the stations got their music programming from a single service company, Bonneville Distribution.

Well, I told myself, *I can keep calling hundreds of stations, or I can go right to the source.*

Once I got the program director for easy-listening music at Bonneville Distribution on the phone, he confirmed that he chose the music for hundreds of stations across the country.

"I wrote a song that I think you're going to love," I told him. "When my local station plays it, listeners light up their phone lines! Could I send you a copy?"

"Well," he said after a pause, "I don't usually talk directly with musical artists, but if the song is half as good as you say it is, I'd be willing to at least give it a listen."

I sent him "Rachel's Song"—then held my breath. Once again, let me put this situation in context with the time period. Today, I'd simply send a file or link to my song online. But at this point, "snail mail" had to do.

Then, after I sent him the 45-rpm record, I had to wait patiently for his response.

I guess I should say I *should have* waited patiently. Instead, I waited somewhat impatiently, full of excitement and anticipation.

Then he called me back.

"I listened to 'Rachel's Song,'" he began in a neutral voice. "And I have to say…" he started, as my heart pounded in my chest, "I absolutely love it! I'm going to add it to the playlist of the stations that come to us for programming."

Boom! In one fell swoop, "Rachel's Song" reached hundreds of radio stations. In no time, the song played in every major market in the United States. I often heard "Rachel's Song" play more than once within the same hour. In fact, Linda and I woke up many times with our clock radio playing "Rachel's Song." And this went on for years.

To this day, a morning WKLM-FM disc jockey, Bill Price, still fondly remembers all the listeners that called in to say how much they loved "Rachel's Song." And I smile when I remember the wonderful times I had during each of my several personal appearances with Bill on the air. With each appearance I reflected on how honored I was to be a part of the momentum, as "Rachel's Song" had launched beyond my wildest dreams.

How Would "Rachel's Song" Sound on a Harp?

One of my favorite places to eat in Nashville in the evenings was the Opryland Hotel and Resort. The resort was home to several great restaurants and an enormous indoor rainforest garden in the atrium, complete with waterfalls. It was stunning. During one of my visits there for work, I met a talented entertainer named Lloyd Lindroth, who played popular songs on his harp every night in the atrium. But he didn't go by Lloyd. His stage name was the Liberace of the Harp, and he dressed the part—playing his harp as flamboyantly as Liberace had played the piano.

His harp music was like a pied piper, attracting the guests closer to hear the music, which echoed throughout the atrium. One evening, I told him about "Rachel's Song" and gave him a cassette copy. The next time I saw Lloyd, he told me that he was so taken by the music that he wanted me to let him play his own arrangement of "Rachel's Song" on the harp.

"Of course," I said without hesitation. "I would even be happy to loan you my 2-inch studio master recording, so that you can make your own accompaniment recording minus the piano to play along with."

After that, each time I saw Lloyd at Opryland, he told the audience he wanted to play a wonderful song named "Rachel's Song." Both his audience and I loved his arrangement.

As "Rachel's Song" was heard more around the country on the radio, I was contacted by other harp players who wanted to perform the song. One talented harpist, Angi Bemiss, was so touched by "Rachel's Song" that she asked me for permission to create and publish a beautiful harp arrangement. Angi later told me that my saying yes to her was the single ah-ha moment that began her now very successful harp arrangement publishing business called Simply the Harp. Thus began an over twenty-year friendship with Angi.

What More Can I Do to Share "Rachel's Song"?

As the popularity of "Rachel's Song" grew, radio stations near and far invited me as a guest on their programs. Back in Winston-Salem, North Carolina, the most popular radio personality (1979–2007) in the area was Glen Scott on WSJS-AM. He always started out playing "Rachel's Song," and then the two of us would tell stories about the music and take calls from listeners. Nationally syndicated host for ABC Satellite Network Radio, Joe Lacina, interviewed me more than once, and I always enjoyed hearing his deep, resonant voice.

The song kept spreading—as did my media appearances. Legendary York, Pennsylvania, broadcaster "Doc" Daugherty, conducted an on-air interview with me. During the interview, he told listeners about the fan mail and phone calls that poured into him each time he played "Rachel's Song" on his two-hour morning "music and trivia" program on WOYK-AM.

Looking for Radio Towers

Naïve musicians (like me in the beginning) often think "making it" is about creating a beautiful song, and letting others do the work of getting it out to the masses. But like any seasoned entrepreneur knows, unless you happen upon a once-in-a-million discovery (with odds less favorable than winning the lottery), achieving musical success is not usually that simple. Along with the creativity required to master a song, musical artists must possess a lot of "hustle" if they want to get discovered—and even more if they actually want to sell their work.

Fortunately, from a young age, I'd known such hard work. I wasn't afraid to introduce my music to others—over and over again.

Since my work at AT&T kept me travelling around the country, I kept my ears open for other easy-listening radio stations. When I found one, I would send them a 45 record to get airplay. When traveling by car, I kept my eyes open, looking for radio station towers—the same thing that Loretta Lynn did in the movie, *Coal Miner's Daughter*. Once I tracked down the radio station, I'd give them one of my records and ask them to play it on the radio.

One day in 1986, out in the countryside near Hillsville, Virginia, I drove up on a small radio station with a tower out back. While I had been keeping my ears open, this time I happened to keep my eyes open too! The letters on the front of the building said WHHV. I stopped, entered their doors, and gave a 45-rpm record of "Rachel's Song" to one of the only two people at the station. Sure enough, the next week, while driving up the mountain to Virginia to work with one of my customers, I tuned in to the Hillsville station, AM 1400, and heard the young woman announcer say, "Now I'm going to play my favorite song. It's called 'Rachel's Song.'"

While I was the person who had played and written the song onto paper, I never lost my belief that God had composed it. Any glory belonged to Him.

I'm not exaggerating; I nearly drove off the road in my excitement!

My thoughts upon hearing "Rachel's Song" on the radio—whether in my hometown, within a bustling big city, or in the mountains of Virginia—were not about me as the composer. While I was the person who had played and written the song onto paper, I never lost my belief that God had composed it. Any glory belonged to Him.

Since God had entrusted me with this music, I felt it was my job to share it with the world. When the song was shared, its love and energy could touch other people's lives—creating their own Godwinks. I continued hearing from many of them. Their letters and phone calls told me how much the song had touched them. I suspected there were many more listeners who stayed silent, but were equally moved.

It didn't matter how many times I heard my song on the radio; each time made me stop in my tracks. To say I was grateful and humbled to be a part of this movement would be a vast understatement. I was reverent. I had been a vessel for something greater than anything I could create alone.

The Parable of the Talents: Investing in My Music from a Young Age

I thought about the parable Jesus told in Matthew about a master giving talents to three of his servants to invest. Two of the servants invested; the third buried his talent. The lesson to me was to invest wisely.

Talents, in the biblical reference, meant money. But to me the lesson of the parable would be the same as if talents represented skills—whether in music, painting, sculpting, public speaking, dance, writing, athleticism, leadership, or any other talent you could name.

I had been given "talents," and it was up to me to invest them wisely.

I reflected on where those talents had come from. God had given me my musical talent, clearly. My parents had provided the resources, encouragement, and support—which helped anchor me in the philosophy of using my talents daily.

By the time I reached five-years-old, Mama and Daddy had bought their first house, which had a living room big enough for a piano. One of their first purchases was a used upright piano with a sweet, angelic sound. While both Mama and Daddy loved music and played all the time, my daddy would rather play the piano than eat.

Even before buying the piano, whenever we would go anywhere with a piano, Daddy would head straight for the piano and start playing. Many times, Daddy did much more playing than visiting whoever we were there to see—sometimes to the dismay of my mama.

Music was part of my everyday life. At home, Daddy would often set me on his knee and let me "bang around" on the piano keys while he played beautiful songs, mostly hymns. In addition to hymns, he knew a few popular songs—and some fun songs that he either learned in school or from his mother. As soon as I learned to talk, he taught me to sing along and play simple notes right along with him.

As I reflected on my upbringing, I believed God had used experiences and people to shape me, like when my daddy looked lovingly at me while I played, as he sat next to me on the bench at home. I believed that God opened certain doors and closed others throughout my life for a purpose. Up until this point, I could see how He guided me to the right field of study, my job at AT&T, my wife Linda, and my love of music. I knew He entrusted me with "Rachel's Song" and wanted me to share it with the world—and I would not bury or squander that "talent."

What more can I do, Lord? I asked Him.

Then, I listened.

CHAPTER FIVE

"Rachel's Song" Makes a Ripple in the Symphony and Beyond

"I know God has inspired you to write or compose this music by the way it has ministered to me—beautiful peace truly comes through."
~PAULA

" Rachel's Song" became bigger than I could have imagined. Like a pebble dropped into the still waters of a lake, which starts out as a small ripple and eventually reaches the entire lake, the song expanded its reach well beyond my control. What had started as a private moment between God and myself as the music played through me had taken on a life of its own—with people I'd never met listening and letting me know how this song impacted them. The further the song traveled, the wider and wider its ripple became.

Through it all, the encouragement of others motivated me to continue driving forward—delivering the song to as many ears as possible.

While the song took on a life of its own, I considered the steps I'd need to ensure that it could continue touching the hearts and lives of people for a long time. From my training and experience as a businessperson, I knew that meant I'd need to ensure I did everything possible to both protect and position my music for future success.

Registering "Rachel's Song" with BMI

Around that time, I heard about the music licensing organizations BMI (Broadcast Music Incorporated) and ASCAP (American Society of Composers, Authors and Publishers). In fact, the first time I had learned they existed was when I drove up and down Music Square in Nashville and saw their logos on their headquarters buildings. I knew what I needed to do.

While in Nashville on business in September 1986, I walked into the BMI office building and approached the receptionist at the front desk.

"Hi," she said with a cheery smile and the familiar, distinct Tennessee accent. "How can I help you today?"

I returned her greeting with a smile of my own. "Hello…I hope you can point me in the right direction. I have written and recorded a song. Now I'd like to talk with someone about how to protect it."

"You've come to the right place!" She smiled as she rose from her chair. "Let me take you to see Phil Graham. I think he's the person you want to talk to."

She walked me around the corner to a small office and introduced me to Phil Graham. I judged Phil to be around thirty years old. Like almost everyone I'd met in the music industry, Phil exuded warmth and friendliness. I counted myself fortunate, once again, feeling that I was under a wing of protection—guiding me to the right people. Perhaps their smiles were another Godwink, letting me know I was on the right track.

Phil rose to shake my hand. "Please, come in and have a seat. I'm in writer-publisher relations. How can I help you?"

I took a few minutes to tell Phil about my recording of "Rachel's Song."

"What would you advise?" I asked, regarding protection of the song.

"Let's go listen to it first," he said. "I want to hear it!" I supposed he must be curious, based on the history of the song I'd shared so far.

Phil walked me down the hall to the boardroom where, as you would expect from a music business, premium sound equipment lined the walls. *I guess it won't be hard to find a way to play the song here*, I thought as the music started quickly after our arrival. Gone were the days of having to scramble for a tape recorder to play my song!

As soon as "Rachel's Song" began to play and the notes echoed softly off the acoustically optimized boardroom, Phil's body shifted. His shoulders relaxed more deeply into his chair. He closed his eyes. He looked lost in the music, totally taken by it.

"Okay," he said, slowly sucking in a deep breath once the song finished playing. "I don't have words to describe that song." He paused before continuing, reinforcing his speechlessness. "…But wow. Let's go back to my office and get you set up."

I was honored, yet again. This man was no stranger to masterful music. *Another one touched by the music*, I thought to myself.

Little could I imagine at that moment that I would eventually register nearly 200 songs with BMI.

Back in his office, we got down to business. He helped me fill out the forms necessary to join BMI as a writer and publisher and to register "Rachel's Song."

Little could I imagine at that moment that I would eventually register nearly 200 songs with BMI. And as far as Phil, I was not surprised that he stayed with BMI, topping off his stellar career as senior vice president of writer-publisher relations. In 2020, I reconnected with Phil, thanking him for his guidance and advice over the years.

"Rachel's Song" Gets Introduced to a Whole Symphony of Musicians

With the music protected, the small ripple was reaching further and further, and along the way, I was witnessing "Rachel's Song" begin to take on a life of its own. As the song spread, the number of highly respected music professionals appreciating it grew.

One such professional resided not far from my home. In November 1986, I visited Peter Perret, the conductor and music director of the Winston-Salem Symphony, at his home in Winston-Salem.

"Peter," I said, "thank you so much for seeing me today. I wonder if you would do me the honor of listening to a song I wrote."

So many of my introductions to "Rachel's Song" had started with this innocent and sincere request: *would you listen to my song?* Maybe the biblical principle, "You have not because you ask not," had been ingrained in me. Or maybe I'd simply learned from sales that by asking, I could open doors. After all, instead of asking God for something, I was simply suggesting that people listen to a beautiful song! Whatever the reason for my success, this simple question seemed to work!

"Sure," he said with a smile. Because of his musical pedigree and expertise, I figured he had been asked a similar favor by many others who'd written a tune. But I wanted his opinion as a professional in the music industry, someone accustomed to leading musicians in playing some of the most beautiful music ever written.

Not long into the song, I witnessed a pattern that had become quite familiar to me: I could see from Peter's expressions that the music moved him emotionally.

"Dave," Peter told me once the music stopped, "you need to get this song arranged for symphony. And when you do, the Winston-Salem Symphony will perform it."

I was floored. I'd hoped for his approval—maybe a small compliment and even a scrap of sage advice. I never expected such a generous offer. I could never have dreamed he'd respond that way!

"You've got a deal!" I said with hearty appreciation. "So, let me ask you, who would you recommend I get to arrange this song for symphony?"

"Fred Tanner," he said instantly. "He's very busy, which is because he's the best. But I highly recommend him. Dr. Tanner is the chairman of the music department at Winston-Salem State University (WSSU)." I absorbed each of his words, and I knew my next move.

Later that day, I phoned Dr. Fred Tanner's office and told him that Peter Perret had recommended him to me. That was all he needed to hear. *I was in.*

"Peter?" he said immediately. "He's a great guy. If Peter sent you my way, I'd be happy to see you. Come on over. Do you have time *now?*"

Another Godwink: I had nowhere else pressing to be. I *did* have time!

As I entered Dr. Tanner's office, I saw walls lined with bookshelves full of music and more stacks of music on his desk.

"Please, have a seat," he said as he greeted me warmly, immediately making me feel welcome and comfortable.

"Thank you, Dr. Tanner," I answered.

"Please call me Fred," he responded in his signature, humble manner. "How can I help you, Dave?"

"I wrote this song called 'Rachel's Song,'" I began, "and after I played it for Peter, he thought I should see you about having the song arranged for symphony." As I spoke the words, I almost couldn't believe where I was—and what I was asking. Everything was falling together in a way that I could never have orchestrated by myself.

"Okay," Fred nodded. "Well, let's have a listen, shall we?" He extended his hand to take the cassette I held.

Here we go again, I thought, bracing myself to watch his response. While my confidence built with each expert who approved of the music, there was always the slim possibility that someone could come back with criticism!

Not in this case...

As soon as he hit the play button, Fred responded much in the same way that Peter had. *Another one touched by the music*, I thought—a little relieved, very honored, and not terribly surprised.

When the song finished playing, Fred took a deep breath. "I'm finding myself in a tough position because of this song of yours," he said. "I really don't have time to do this, but I feel like I have to do this arrangement for you."

I tried not to fall out of my chair. "Really?" I asked. I trusted it was *real*, but compulsively I had to ask, sort of like pinching oneself to be sure what's being witnessed is not a dream. "Well, I don't know what to say. But thank you *so very much*. That is just...wonderful!" My words fell short of expressing just how grateful I was for the opportunity, but Fred seemed satisfied with my response. We made tentative arrangements for how we would proceed.

What a confirmation! Both a professional conductor and a professional music professor gave me such a positive response on the same day! I was in disbelief. *This is it!* I thought to myself as I left his office.

Shortly after Christmas, I got a call from Fred.

"Dave, I have your arrangement of 'Rachel's Song,'" he said. "Care to come back to my office?"

I don't even remember if I hung up the phone, but I know I raced to Fred's office at WSSU.

"Here you go, Dave," he said as he handed me the arrangement— handwritten—the conductor's score, ten pages on long 11" by 17" paper, with each instrument's music neatly written on a separate music staff.

"I can almost hear it now," I said with gusto. "Again, Fred, I can't thank you enough. How does it sound?" I asked.

"I haven't heard it played by an orchestra. But from what I've heard in my head, I love it," he laughed.

"My goodness!" I gushed. "What talent! That's what happened when I sat down at the piano. I just heard the song in my head. Now, Fred, what do I owe you for this?"

"Nothing," he waved his hand.

"No, sir," I protested. "I don't think I could live with myself if I didn't pay you for your time and talents. Please, just tell me what I can pay," I begged.

"No," he shook his head emphatically. "I won't take a penny. This was just something I had to do for this song," he said.

For this song, I thought, letting those words hang in the air. Again, it was as if the song had its own life, and others were compelled to protect and nurture it.

"Surely there is something I can do to thank you, Fred," I pleaded.

"Well yes...there is something," he finally relented. "Make sure you invite me to hear it performed by the Winston-Salem Symphony," he said.

Done, I thought—and said. But first, I had somewhere to go....

I drove directly to Peter Perret's house and showed him the conductor's score. As he looked through the music, I could tell that, like Fred, he was playing it over in his head.

"Oooooh, I like it! I want to schedule this as part of the Valentine's Day concert in February," he said.

The ripple was widening once again.

"Wonderful! What do I need to do now?" I asked.

Peter gave me homework. He asked me to make a separate copy of the music for each of the twenty-four different instruments in the symphony. And I have to say, even using the music software on my computer, it still took me many hours to input the music from Dr. Tanner's handwritten score, note-by-note, for each instrument. Once I finished, I made the copies and delivered them to the symphony office.

Conductor's Score for Rachel's Song

Peter invited Linda and me to attend the symphony rehearsal Saturday night before the Valentine's Day performance the next day. The short, fifteen-minute drive to the symphony rehearsal room on Coliseum Drive was filled with excitement and anticipation. Even before we reached the entrance door to the room, we could hear the familiar sound of the musicians warming up—the discordant yet somehow beautiful sound of multiple instruments simultaneously playing different songs. Peter greeted us warmly as we entered the room. He immediately introduced us to Elaine Richey, first chair violinist and concertmaster. Remember that last name, as it will return later in this book.

Elaine was everything you would expect in a first-class musician—elegant, poised, neatly dressed with beautiful wavy hair, friendly yet very serious about her music. The other musicians obviously respected her leadership.

I watched with fascination as Elaine took her copy of "Rachel's Song" and began marking it for her violin bow strokes (down bows and up bows) as she played through the song.

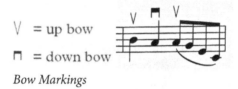

Bow Markings

When she finished, all of the other first violin musicians gathered around her chair and copied Elaine's bow markings on their own music. The other stringed instrument musicians did the same for their parts.

Witnessing this, I understood how all the musicians in the orchestra were so perfectly synchronized in their motions.

As the rehearsal began, Peter graciously introduced Linda and me to the orchestra and told the story of how moved he was when I first played "Rachel's Song" at his home. He also said how pleased he was with Fred Tanner's arrangement for symphony.

We settled in as the music began. Linda and I watched in absolute awe as Peter conducted the symphony. They played "Rachel's Song" perfectly, the first time through. I'd heard the song play hundreds of times at this point—but never quite like this. This night was a gift to me, to observe their masterful performance of that once-private little song.

What an incredibly beautiful sound! What talent these musicians possess! My thoughts expressed every exemplary praise I could think of, as I beamed and soaked up the scene. I wanted to stretch out the moment, to hear it again.

They had only seen the music for a few minutes before playing it, yet they mastered it quickly. Compared to their usually challenging classical music, "Rachel's Song" was very easy for them. Fred Tanner's arrangement stayed true in every way to the original recording by Gary Prim.

After the first time through the song, Peter suggested one little addition to the music score. At the dramatic point when the orchestra timpani and cymbals built up to a crescendo for the sudden key change from C to D flat, Peter added the subtle but distinctive sound of a bell tree, which reminded me of the sound I'd heard years before in the *Cinderella* movie, when the fairy godmother waved her magic wand.

I talked to Peter after the rehearsal, and he had a surprise for me.

"Dave, how would you like to conduct the symphony performing your music?"

That nearly knocked me off my feet—I was not expecting that wonderful gesture at all. Overwhelmed by his generosity, I gave him an unequivocal and instantaneous, "Yes! To be honest, that is something I've always dreamed of doing!"

The Benton Convention Center where the Valentine's Day event was to be held had sold out the convention floor seats for the performance. In the back of my mind, I wanted a good recording of this once-in-a-lifetime performance. I hauled along my heavy, reel-to-reel Sony tape recorder, and the event sound engineers plugged it into the main soundboard so I could get a tape recording of the performance. Our local NBC television station, WXII, also came along with their recording and video equipment. When it came time for my part on the program, Peter graciously introduced me as the composer. He also recognized and thanked Dr. Fred Tanner, seated at our table, as the arranger of this symphonic version of "Rachel's Song."

After the introductions, Peter invited me up to the stage. Once I got there, he looked me in the eye, smiled, held out his baton, flipped it over, and elegantly presented it to me—handle first, in the perfect position to conduct the symphony. I stepped up onto the conductor's podium and took my position at the "best seat in the house"!

Before I moved the baton, I savored the moment, letting it wash over me. *What a privilege to conduct these talented musicians.* I had conducted many choirs before since I was in high school, all throughout college, and at my local church for years. But this experience—facing a professional, seventy-five-piece orchestra—raised my adrenaline to a new level. Slowly, I raised the baton—

> **Each musician followed every movement of my baton and body language as if we had worked together for years.**

all musicians' eyes locked on me—gave ever so brief a pause as I looked toward the violins, then started my 4/4-time downbeat for the violins to play the introduction.

Each musician followed every movement of my baton and body language as if we had worked together for years. The music surrounded me, and it entered my ears like a chorus of angels. Talk about "surround sound." As each subtle and pronounced note played—from the delicate stringed instruments to the brass tuba, French horn, and trombone—the heavenly sounds that stroked my ears was true *surround sound*.

When the last strains of "Rachel's Song" faded away, and the last clear note sounded on the triangle musical instrument, the next sounds I heard as I turned toward the audience were thunderous applause—accompanied by a spontaneous standing ovation. With tears of joy in my eyes and a big smile on my face, I gave a slow, deep bow of genuine appreciation to the audience. I saw the smiles of joy from so many friends in the audience—especially Linda, Bob McHone, and Fred Tanner sitting at our table. Then I turned to my right toward Elaine Richey as concertmaster, and I walked over and shook her hand, giving a slight bow in appreciation.

The applause got louder.

Then I motioned with both hands raised, palm upward, for the entire orchestra to rise.

As they did, the applause grew even louder.

I turned back to the audience, gave one last bow of thanks, and walked off the stage—handing the baton, handle first, back to Peter Perret as we shook hands.

Peter had just one word for me, "Wonderful!" The standing ovation had lasted over a minute from the audience of a couple thousand people.

It was mind-boggling to think that a mere song played alone in my home had turned into *this*. This experience felt like a lifetime achievement to me. *Would there be more to come? Or was this it?* I left the convention center that night satisfied—with whatever the future held. "Rachel's Song" already had touched so many people—including me.

The WXII-TV NBC station manager kindly shared with me the raw video footage of the entire performance that day. That gift allowed me to relive this special moment many times over the years. I still especially enjoy hearing the symphony recording while sitting at my piano and playing along, thus turning it into my own private piano concerto.

CHAPTER SIX

"Rachel's Song" Goes Around the World

"Thank you for the beautiful music you've brought into our home! My children and I have been through a horrible crisis, and so many days and nights your music has brought peace and relaxation into our minds and hearts."
~CAROLE

When God is the conductor of my life, meaningful connections form in the oddest of places. I never want to interrupt His work—but rather to join His orchestra and play the part He's assigned to me. He always does the rest, as long as I follow His cues.

In 1986, Linda worked in Raleigh, North Carolina, as then-Governor James Martin's education advisor. One day after work, she stopped at a gas station on her way home, but the gas pump kept acting up. A man on the other side of the pump offered to help her.

"Hi," he said, "I'm Steve Robertson."

Linda and Steve struck up a conversation, and Linda learned that Steve had recently returned to the United States after working for several years in Australian television. He shared that he wanted to teach. Since Linda had several friends in education circles, she offered to meet with him again to make some introductions. The two exchanged contact information and went their separate ways.

Later, Steve visited Linda at her office. Somehow, the conversation turned to music—then my music, and eventually "Rachel's Song."

God was conducting, yet again.

Linda played the song for Steve in the car on their way to lunch.

"Wow...I love it!" Linda was not surprised by his response—yet as we always were when someone new appreciated "Rachel's Song," she was honored. "My favorite tunes are those with a compelling melody like this song has. This is clearly a tune that will go somewhere." Steve had been around plenty of high-quality music—and professional musicians. His opinion was not that of an amateur.

His opinion was not that of an amateur.

One thing led to another. Steve's girlfriend back in Australia came for a visit over Christmas vacation, and they stayed in our home with us. Such lovely people. We enjoyed getting to know them both. I learned even more about Steve. It turned out he was a jazz music expert, both a writer and teacher, with many media connections in Australia.

After dinner, we played "Rachel's Song" for them, which they both just loved.

And yes, this story is *going somewhere!*

Since Steve first met Linda, he had been offered a job back in Perth, Western Australia, to teach broadcast journalism, which he had happily accepted. Fast-forward a few months. Once Steve got settled back in Australia, he contacted the music director at 2CH 1170 AM, an easy-listening station in Sydney, and sent them a copy of "Rachel's Song" that I had given him before he left the United States. The station put the song on the air immediately. The reaction was much the same as it was the first time it was played on WKLM-FM. Listeners responded, asking about the song, letting the station know how it had touched them—reinforcing that they too were *touched by the music.* The station played it every day. It really took off in popularity. All the many people who wrote the station to ask about "Rachel's Song" were referred to Steve. Steve, being the kind and helpful friend that he was, responded to each one of the fans and told them how to order the music from Combs Music in the United States. How exciting for us to go to the mailbox and find envelopes with wonderful letters and orders for "Rachel's Song" from Australia.

God clearly wasn't done conducting.

More than two years later, in 1989, Steve was talking with the music director at 2CH Radio, who informed him that "Rachel's Song" was the most popular requested instrumental on their station for at least the last two years.

As an interesting aside, I learned that the "CH" in 2CH stands for churches. Since the beginning in 1932, the 2CH radio license was owned by the New South Wales (NSW) Council of Churches. I had no idea that there was a religious connection with this radio station. Many of the thousands of Christians who listened to 2CH radio became loyal fans of my music.

A sister radio station, 6KY AM 1206—2,400 miles away in Perth on the east coast of Australia—played "Rachel's Song" and got a similar response. I think that it is another Godwink that 6KY is now 94.5 FM in Perth, the exact same frequency of WKLM-FM in Greensboro, North Carolina, where "Rachel's Song" was played on the radio for the very first time.

Dave's Music Goes to the Movies

Yet another coincidence, or Godwink? I'll let you decide, regarding this next event. Once, when Linda was on a business trip to Washington, DC, she met a man named Dick Guttman, a successful "publicist for the stars" back in Hollywood. Dick's reaction to hearing "Rachel's Song" was that it sounded to him like a theme song to a movie, particularly a love story.

He wasn't the first to tell me that. In fact, I'd heard that many times before. But no one with his connections had ever said it!

Dick put me in touch with the music people at United Artists, who were in the early stages of planning a new James Bond movie, *The Living Daylights*. Thanks to Dick's connections, United Artists asked me to submit some of my original music for their upcoming movie. Linda and I love James Bond movies, and my excitement level at getting this invitation to be a part of the movie's creation was off the charts.

United Artists even sent me an advance copy of the movie synopsis script, so I could get the general outline and feel of the story. This script proved to be great inspiration for the writing of the song I would submit.

But that isn't all there was to this story. God was cueing up other parts of the orchestra to join in....

Before composing any music to send, I called my high school friend and multi-talented musician, Stan Moon, who lived in Kentucky. After telling him all about the opportunity, Stan and his wife, Carmon, felt inspired (cue: musicians!) and wrote some great lyrics. Once I received their lyrics, I too got inspired and composed the music for the song, which we titled, "Danger in Your Love."

I wasted no time calling Gary Prim about "Danger in Your Love"—the original piece that Stan, Carmon, and I had written.

"And by the way, Gary," I added, "I have also written two other new songs that I would *love* to have you arrange and record."

"That's wonderful," he said as cheerfully as always. Gary had proven to be a very supportive person—both to me and my music—so he was the first person I considered for this role. "We might as well do it all at the same time. You know the drill! If you send me the lead sheets, I'll get ready for the recording session." I heard the smile in his voice and believed he might be as excited as I was.

Gary recommended that this time, we use a studio called Reflections located in the Berry Hill suburb of Nashville. Gary liked the way the Yamaha grand piano at Reflections played and sounded. Gary also suggested using Ronny Light as our recording engineer. Moving forward, both Gary and Ronny would become lifelong friends to Linda and me.

I called Gene Lawson, the owner of Reflections, and booked three four-hour sessions of studio time in Studio A for Friday, February 27, 1987. When I told Gene the kind of music we would be recording with Gary, Stan, and Ronny, he said that he would have the piano freshly tuned for our session. Talk about great customer service! Not only was God conducting the orchestra of my life, but he was ensuring that the environment the music was played in would be superb as well!

This time, Linda came with me to Nashville. It had been only a short six months since I'd watched and listened as "Rachel's Song" was recorded. No longer would I scramble to find a way to play a song for her from hundreds of miles away—or long for her to witness the splendor of the recording studio scene I was honored to see. No, this time, she would be my *partner* in it all—not just supporting me emotionally from afar, but physically there to enjoy it! I was beyond thrilled, and I hoped she would find the experience as inspiring as I had.

"I'm sorry you missed the session when 'Rachel's Song' got recorded," I told Linda, "but today's session will be just as memorable. I promise!"

I trusted God would help me deliver on that promise!

Inspiration in Studio A

Studio A at Reflections consisted of two rooms—a control room and a large, soundproof studio room much like the one at the Music Mill studio. We gathered in the control room, where Gene introduced us to Ronny Light—the friendly, soft-spoken recording engineer. I immediately loved that Ronny seemed just as excited about our recording session as we were.

Ronny set up the microphones for the piano and prepared the tape machines and console. Two other young men brought in and set up Gary's synthesizer equipment.

A few minutes later, Stan and Carmon Moon entered the studio, with Stan carrying his guitar case. And right behind them was Gary Prim. After I made some quick introductions, Gary and Carmon made their way to the piano in the main studio room and started rehearsing the arrangement Gary had written. The consummate professional, Gary, immediately found the right key for the song to perfectly match Carmon's vocal range.

Carmon entered the vocal isolation booth on the left side of the studio. Once she closed the door, we could see her, and she could see us, but the only way she could hear any sound was through her headphones. The rest of us stayed back in the control room with Ronny.

I glanced over at Linda, who appeared to be enjoying the experience as much as I had enjoyed that first recording. *God is delivering on that promise!* I thought, as the music began.

The recording process finished quickly, requiring only a few takes to get the basic piano and vocal tracks done. Once those tracks were complete, Ronny set up a microphone in the studio to record Stan playing his acoustic guitar, which would serve as an interlude between the first and second verses. Then, to put the finishing touches on the recording, Gary went to his synthesizer keyboard and added some

We all thought that the song had the sound, feel, and story elements of the perfect theme song for the James Bond movie, *The Living Daylights*.

deep, low strings—then some high strings, and an occasional electric piano fill on his Yamaha DX-7 synthesizer.

Once all tracks were mixed, Ronny played it back for us over the monitor speakers in the control room. We all thought that the song had the sound, feel, and story elements of the perfect theme song for the James Bond movie, *The Living Daylights*.

Here are the lyrics:
"Danger in Your Love"
Lyrics by: Stan and Carmon Moon

First Verse:
From the first I knew I loved you.
You passed by without a glance.
Will I ever get to hold you?
Does our love have even one chance?

Chorus:
There is danger in your love.
There is risk in your embrace.
Is there someone else you love?
Will you leave without a trace?

Unknown pleasure in your arms.
Time for us is slipping by.
Is your love the kind that harms?
Will we kiss before we die?
Come and hold me in your arms.

Instrumental Interlude:

Second Verse:
I'll face the danger in your love.
Let's give up this game we play.
Make this promise oh my love.
In my arms you'll always stay.

Repeat Chorus

Lyrics © 1986 Stan Moon and Carmon Moon, Used by Permission

The Birth of Two New Songs

While the primary purpose for this recording session was to record "Danger in Your Love," I sent Gary the lead sheets for a couple of other new songs I had written. Thanks to Gary's ability to create such impressive work in such a limited amount of time, we had plenty of studio time left to record these other songs. In no time, Gary recorded his arrangements of these new songs. As he had done earlier, he laid down the piano track before adding strings and other instruments on the synthesizer. The first of the two new songs had a more upbeat tempo. While I liked Gary's arrangement of this song, I decided later that it didn't quite blend with the other songs, so it *hit the cutting room floor*, as they say.

But the second new song was another story. It sounded great. It was in a minor key, and the low and high strings that Gary added were perfect. This new song would be named "Symphony of Peace" and would become the second track on the "Rachel's Song" album—and a fan favorite.

Linda and I soaked up the quality time with everyone in the studio. Again, I felt honored and blessed by the experience—and especially grateful Linda had been by my side for it all. At suppertime, we were joined by Gary Prim's wonderful wife, Julie, to wrap up a successful day.

Heading to Hollywood

With "Danger in Your Love" in hand and an introduction to a young United Artists representative, I flew to Los Angeles, California, in early March of 1987. He and I arranged to have lunch at the iconic Hard Rock Café in Hollywood.

"I can't wait to hear what you've come up with," the young man told me as we waited for our lunch to be served.

I got out my Sony Walkman cassette player (remember, this was before cell phones and streaming music gave us instant, easy access to nearly any song on the planet!) and handed him the headphones. I pushed play, and like many times before, I waited for his response. Except this time, it wasn't "Rachel's Song"!

As "Danger in Your Love" played privately for his ears amidst the bustling restaurant, he nodded his head up and down in approval.

"I really like what I hear," he said, which was music to my ears, pun intended! I knew my song making the cut on the James Bond movie would be a long shot, but I knew I had to try.

"Of course, I can't make you any promises," he told me. "We will be hearing from several artists before the director, Cubby Broccoli, makes his decision. But I promise I will be in touch with you as soon as I can with an answer."

Several weeks later, the representative from United Artists called me back.

"Everyone who heard your song loved it," he told me. "But the final decision falls to the director, Cubby Broccoli. Unfortunately, he has selected another song he thinks best matches the pacing of the movie."

Sometimes as composer—or perhaps more aptly, in this case, as musical engineer—God adds tracks to my life to make it even greater. Other times, God cuts out what doesn't belong—leaving those portions on the cutting room floor. As the composer, producer, and engineer of my life, God knew what fit best; I simply needed to trust Him.

I later learned Cubby chose the Norwegian rock band, A-ha! I guess if I had to lose out to someone, it might as well be A-ha! In any case, I felt that it was a real honor just to be asked to submit my music. After all, I learned a lot and enjoyed a great trip to Hollywood. I guess you could say that this experience was another "A-ha" moment of a different sort (pun intended, yet again!).

But great things even come out of situations that don't go our way. Sometimes the portions on the cutting room floor of life get used and lead to something else of greater significance. For example, writing and recording "Danger in Your Love" brought me back together with Stan Moon. We had been close friends and fellow Explorer Scouts in high school, and our friendship had continued through our four years at East Tennessee State University. But as often happens, after graduation, our lives took us in different directions. Stan and I had only seen each other in previous years at high school class reunions. I realized just how blessed I was to have Stan and his musical talents with me.

Once again, the talents God had bestowed were being invested, and I could see their growth over time.

"Rachel's Song" Gets Prepped for the Piano Players Everywhere

Going back to those high school days with Stan Moon, music played a strong role in my life. Whenever I'd hear a song on the radio with a catchy piano part, I would buy the piano sheet music so I could learn to play it for myself.

In 1960, I heard "Last Date" by Floyd Cramer for the first time. *He knows his way around a keyboard,* I thought, a bit mesmerized while listening to his distinctive slides on the piano—which became his signature style. I, and a lot of other people, loved to imitate him.

Then in 1969 came Henry Mancini's hit recording of "A Time for Us," the theme song from the movie *Romeo and Juliet*. I experienced love at first hearing with that song—and apparently so did everyone else.

For me, putting my hands on new sheet music from the music store was like finding a new treasure. I couldn't wait to get to the nearest piano to play it.

As I thought about how Gary Prim had played "Rachel's Song," I thought about how much I would love to have it transcribed the same way Gary had played it during the recording. *If I had that sheet music,* I told myself, *I could play along with Gary's recording—note-for-note—and so could everybody else.*

I'd brought home enough sheet music in my day to know that many artists sold sheet music that did not really match the recording—different key, notes missing, and overly simplified. When I noticed the discrepancy, I'd say to myself, *if I ever produce any sheet music, I will have it meticulously transcribed note-for-note to match any recording I produce.*

So that's what I decided to do! I spent hours and hours over many months transcribing "Rachel's Song" by ear—note-for-note, measure by measure. I would play the song on my Sony Walkman cassette player, write down the piano notes I heard, then play each measure as I heard it over and over again—until I was satisfied that my transcription of the song aligned 100 percent with what Gary had recorded.

Once I created a handwritten copy of the song, I used a music engraving software application called Professional Composer, which ran on my Apple computer. From my handwritten transcription, I spent many hours carefully putting "Rachel's Song" into my computer—note by note. When I was finished, I had a professional-looking version of the music of "Rachel's Song."

I wasn't done with that sheet music project yet. I created a simple cover and put the story behind the writing and naming of "Rachel's Song" on the back of the sheet music. I then took the layout of the sheet music to my friends, Gary and Vicky Bell, who owned Bell Printing. They gladly printed 100 copies for me.

First Page of "Rachel's" Song Sheet Music

Once I had those printed copies in hand, I got back to my other sort of hustling: it was time to get this music into the hands of those who could use—and sell—it. I immediately visited the three music stores in Winston-Salem in 1987—Reznick's Record Store, Separk Music, and Duncan Music. My first stop was to see Mrs. Bee Separk and her daughter, Phyllis, of Separk Music. Mrs. Separk and her departed husband had been instrumental in the founding of the Winston-Salem Symphony many years before and were much beloved by the entire community. She eagerly took as many copies to sell as I would give her. (Separk Music would later play a major role in the life of Combs Music; God's orchestra was growing.)

Next stop was Reznick's Record Store, where I got a similar reception from Mrs. Reznick. Then I went to Duncan Music Company on Stratford Road, where I took my new sheet music in to see Mr. "C.H." Duncan, the owner.

"This looks very professionally done, Dave," he said. "And you got this done fast. Good for you. I'd be happy to sell it here. I sell mostly to high school bands, but we get a good amount of foot traffic from people looking for individual sheet music. Let's see what happens."

"C.H."—like so many along this journey—would later become my good friend.

As it turned out, some fans who heard "Rachel's Song" on the radio wrote to me and wanted the sheet music. I gladly referred them to the best source to purchase it. Putting the sheet music on the Combs Music order form also generated sales of this new form of "Rachel's Song."

Turns out that I was right in thinking that lots of pianists would want to play "Rachel's Song." Combs Music sold over 7,000 copies of the single sheet music.

Around that same time, the North Carolina Federation of Music Clubs (NCFMC) notified me that "Rachel's Song" had received the Social Music Award. This was a big deal. The NCFMC had over 250 clubs all across the state, with over 4,000 members, who were mostly music teachers. The award was given at their annual meeting in Raleigh. I was really moved to see that even the sheet music that I had created for "Rachel's Song" was touching the lives of young musicians.

While "Rachel's Song" remained dear to me, I had other songs in me—or perhaps others that would come straight from God Himself. I just needed the time to sit at my piano and let them flow from my heart to my hands.

CHAPTER SEVEN

REFLECTING ON MY MUSICAL JOURNEY

"Thank you so very much for your beautiful music which creates such an atmosphere of worship and helps us to enter into God's presence."
~CAROL

When you witness a masterful piece of music played—perhaps at your church, through your car's speakers, or at the home of a friend—you may stop and think, Wow, what an amazing song. Few who work outside of the music industry—or any serious art for that matter—likely stop to consider the immense dedication involved to create anything that achieves such a reach. Every inspired song—and songwriter—in fact has a backstory.

Every inspired song—and songwriter—in fact has a backstory.

While I will spare you from hearing all of mine, I do think it's important to get a brief snapshot of how and where I acquired my music passion—and from whom.

"Rachel's Song" wasn't the first song I'd ever played; my music history was as old as I was. Music didn't just happen for me one day; it was a part of my every day, for as long as I could remember. It was *what I did*, and a large part of *who I was*. I will share a bit of those details on my early life, so that as you read about "Rachel's Song," you can put it in context.

The People God Orchestrated to Guide Me

By the time "Rachel's Song" came about, while my mama was still living, my daddy was no longer with me. However, even after his death, I owed my love for music to him—and my mama—who made sure that music was a huge part of my everyday life.

And along the way, others watered that seed of musical passion my parents planted in me.

Growing up in eastern Tennessee, my family may have been relatively poor, but so was pretty much everyone else where we lived! What we lacked in money, we made up for with the ever presence of family, fellowship, and music.

Both Mama and Daddy came from musical families. As a child, Mama walked for miles to take piano lessons from her teacher. And then she walked more miles to her Grandpa McConnell's house to practice on their piano. Daddy played too, mostly by ear.

Both also knew all the old church hymns, and nothing brought our family closer than listening to and playing music together. I can't recall a time when I couldn't play at least a simple song the piano. I imagine as a toddler, I'd sit on my Daddy's lap as he played, and he'd gradually let me learn the notes with him—or perhaps experiment with my own!

God also used Pat Alderman, or Uncle Pat as everyone called him, as another major influence on my life. All through my eight years at Love Chapel Elementary School, Uncle Pat served as our traveling music teacher. From Uncle Pat, I learned all the old, fun campfire songs—like "Home on the Range" and "Oh Susanna." I still find myself singing them to myself while driving or puttering around my home!

Uncle Pat later changed jobs and became my choral teacher all through my years at Unicoi County High School. Tennessee held an all-state chorus competition each year for high school students. My senior year, I was selected as the baritone of an eight-member ensemble, and we got to travel to Nashville along with Uncle Pat. This was a great honor for me—and surely would be a great adventure! One of my classmates that was selected for all-state was our multi-talented Mark Jacoby. Mark's beautiful tenor voice and acting talents would later take him to a successful career on Broadway, where he played the lead role in the musicals, The Phantom of the Opera and Show Boat among others.

I have three distinct memories of that trip. First, I will never forget the sounds of singing with several hundred of the most talented, beautiful young voices from across the state. Second, I remember when our ensemble broke into spontaneous song while eating a meal in a restaurant, much to the delight of the other patrons! I must admit that we sounded really good. And finally, that trip gave me my first experience eating at a Shoney's Big Boy restaurant. That last detail might not seem important, but having grown up in a small town without a lot of exposure to chain restaurants, it was quite memorable to me at the time! Who could have guessed that I'd later be dining in Hollywood at a famous restaurant with movie producers?

Playing Music on the Tropicana Ships

I spent the summer before and my junior year in high school in Bradenton, Florida, where my daddy was working at Tropicana Products. The owner of Tropicana at the time was Anthony Rossi. In addition to being a successful businessman, Mr. Rossi was a strong Baptist who believed in sharing his Christianity through lay ministry. Tropicana had a fleet of ships that would bring oranges from Honduras into the Tampa Bay for offloading and processing in Bradenton. The crews on these ships were from Honduras, and they were pretty much stuck on the ship while in port.

It turned out that Mr. Rossi wanted these crews to have access to a worship service on Sundays. So, after breakfast, Russell Riegler (Mr. Rossi's son-in-law), Daddy, and I volunteered to go out to the ship every Sunday to deliver a Bible lesson in the Tampa Bay Harbor. Daddy would lead the singing of hymns, and I would accompany the singing on an old Estey WWII Chaplin portable pump organ. It had to be portable, so we could haul it up onto the ship and set it up; but at sixty pounds, it was still heavy. Thinking back, that must have been quite a sight to see us lugging that instrument on deck—packed up into a box—to play for a crew of shipmates who were eager for our visit!

I enjoyed our routine once on the ship. The crewmembers would bring me an orange crate to sit on. I would uncrate and unfold the wooden pump organ, preparing myself to supply the leg power to pump the foot petals, which forced air around the organ reeds. The instrument would then produce whichever notes I played on its piano-like keys.

As more of the crew gathered, I could see their friendly and welcoming faces. I knew they loved hearing the music, even though few if any spoke English.

Daddy would stand beside me with his hymnal. When I began playing, with his beautiful voice, he would sing simple hymns such as "Amazing Grace," "The Old Rugged Cross," and "What a Friend We Have in Jesus." Later, Russell would read some Scripture and give a brief Bible lesson in Spanish.

As I folded up the organ and packed it up each visit, the crew would smile, thank us, and go back to their work. We were delighted to bring some musical joy—and a lesson of hope, joy, and redemption to these special shipmates. And Mr. Rossi's devotion further modeled for me how music and service to others worked harmoniously to fulfill God's work.

But I was probably the one who got the most out of these Sunday mornings. I was touched and motivated by the experience each time I played for this audience. And that ship served as my musical training ground.

At the beginning of the summer, I could barely play the hymns. During the week—while Daddy was at work, and when I was not working on my various jobs—I was at the house by myself with no air conditioning, and too hot to go outside. So, I stayed inside playing hymns on the piano! Then I switched to the portable pump organ when I wanted a different sound. I would practice playing every hymn in the hymnbook, six or seven hours a day.

For me, playing music day in and day out didn't seem like work as much as tapping into a greater joy. I've come to believe in developing the talents God offers, not just the ones that seem like they *should* be developed! I don't think wild horses could have kept me from playing, and my God-given passion helped my talent grow. I thank God that my daddy gave me access to those instruments, and that Mr. Rossi provided me the opportunity to use my talents. Where there is motivation, growth happens.

> **For me, playing music day in and day out didn't seem like work as much as tapping into a greater joy.**

Fortunately, my daddy supported my musical talents—and passion—through and through. Sometimes when Daddy got home, we would play music together. Often, we would perform at other churches or retirement villages. I was so motivated by these performances and engagements that by the end of the summer, I could play every hymn in the book. I think it is safe to say that I am the only person who ever learned to play the piano on an old antique portable pump organ on the deck of a Honduran orange juice cargo ship docked in the Tampa Bay Harbor. No doubt, I was *touched by the music* through these special experiences!

But my heart was torn between living in Florida with my daddy and living in Tennessee. I missed being home in the mountains with my mother and brother. After my junior year in high school ended, I went back home to Erwin, Tennessee, and finished my high school senior year.

Jumping Ship to Graduation

As I've hinted earlier in this story, God used other people to make sure I got the best education possible. At my high school graduation ceremony, Principal Leonard Gallimore came to the podium for the presentation of the awards. I had worked hard to earn straight A's in school, but I still wasn't surprised when none of the twelve awards he announced had my name on them.

Then, after clearing his throat, Mr. Gallimore continued, "I have one more award to announce. The Erwin Kiwanis Club has awarded their college scholarship to David Combs."

At first, I thought I'd misheard him. I still tear up thinking about that moment. As I stood up to be recognized, everyone applauded. I looked over toward the bleachers, and I'll never forget the big smile of pride—and probably relief!—on my mama's face. My family did what they could to pay the bills. Funding college for me and my younger brother, Don, had never been within their reach. Thanks to the $800 scholarship loan from the Erwin Kiwanis Club, I would attend and graduate from East Tennessee State University.

Tuition at that time was $55 per quarter. No, that is not a misprint. No zeros missing. Thanks to this low tuition neither I nor my fellow students were saddled with large student loans when we graduated.

I was never sure how I won a scholarship that I didn't know existed. But I have my suspicions about who had helped. Ed and Lucille Hammer served as faithful members of our church, Calvary Baptist. They were long-time choir members, and lifelong family friends. Ed sold insurance and was a member of the Erwin Kiwanis Club. I've rarely known a better example of a wonderful, caring Christian man. Ed and Lucille had no children of their own, and I guess you could say that they adopted me in a way.

These two folks were just a couple of the people from Erwin who showed kindness and generosity without requiring any recognition or a spotlight—just the satisfaction that they were able to help someone in need. That's a lesson I carry with me today.

Another person who God put into my life at the right moment and with the right message—part of the orchestra He'd cast in my success—was a gentleman named Stan Johnson, a professor in the math department at East Tennessee State University. During my senior year of high school, Stan spoke at a school-wide assembly at Unicoi County High School. I held onto every word, as if he were Steve Jobs.

He talked about some new technology they had at the university called a *computer*. As he explained what the computer could do, computing multiple tasks thousands of times faster than human beings, I decided on the spot: *if and when I get to college, I will study computers!* When Stan mentioned that the machine resided in the math department at ETSU and that he was in charge of its use, well, I knew where I needed to go to college! When I got that scholarship, my new goal became possible.

Stan's impact redirected my life. Because of him, I went to ETSU as a math major and physics minor. To help pay for my college expenses not covered by the scholarship, I worked part-time all four years in the university's computer center. Guess who served as my boss? Stan Johnson. He taught me my first two computer-programming courses using Basic and Fortran as the computer languages.

The computer we used was an IBM 1620 with 30K of memory and an electric typewriter that could type ten characters per second for printed output. To put that computer in perspective, the iPhone in my pocket today has over 17 million times that much memory. The programs were all input into the computer using IBM 80-column punch cards. I learned how to punch my own programs using the IBM 029 Card Punch machine.

My primary job in the computer center was to assist graduate students with the supporting computer work, primarily statistical analysis, needed for their graduate theses. At the same time, I took every computer programming and statistics course offered. In fact, I ended up teaching one of the basic programming classes my senior year. That's when I made an interesting discovery: my best computer programming students were music and arts majors.

For the first time, I realized that my own strong interest in music fit right into that pattern.

Between the generosity from folks like the Hammers and leaders like Stan Johnson, once I finished my undergraduate degree at East Tennessee State University, I quickly found a great job developing computer systems for Western Electric—which eventually became AT&T. Because of my education background and four years I'd spent learning, applying, and even teaching computer technology, I didn't have to start working at an entry-level. I had a four-year head start.

At this point you might be wondering if you accidentally picked up the wrong book. Don't worry, I haven't forgotten about "Rachel's Song." I'm coming back to the music. But I shared these stories not only to provide a snapshot of where my musical passion and skills began, but also to make a different point: *If God provided me with such powerful role models and experiences throughout my early years, I knew He would keep guiding me throughout the rest of my life.*

CHAPTER EIGHT

On the Move and Making More Music

"I recently received the album of Rachel's Song (my first taste of your music). My soul took flight! It is truly beautiful, and you have helped make the world a better place. You have a gift, and I am truly happy for you."
~NORMAN

In 1987, while "Rachel's Song" kept growing in popularity, so did my wife Linda's popularity. That fall, duty called once again when President Ronald Reagan asked her to fill a position with the Veterans Administration in Washington, DC.

At about the same time, rumors floated that the AT&T plant where I worked in Winston-Salem might be closing. If that happened, everyone at the plant would either need to move to other plants like Oklahoma City or find a job elsewhere. Several times during our marriage, I had opportunities to move and take promotions with AT&T. Each time, relocating just didn't seem like the right thing to do. But if this plant closure happened, I would have no choice but to move.

Linda had commuted before to jobs in Washington, DC, so we decided it would be best if Linda went ahead and accepted the job in Washington, which she did in October of 1987.

Linda flew to Washington, DC, every Monday morning and returned home Friday evening, while I stayed in North Carolina. During the week, we talked every day on the phone. We spent a lot of time on those evening calls—and in person on weekends—brainstorming about next steps for my music. One thing we knew for certain: the music needed to continue being heard. That meant it needed to continue being played! We let God guide our conversations and hearts, as we considered new doors He might open.

We also were determined to find a way to market my music and get more radio airplay.

About the same time, I got my first quarterly BMI royalty check from radio airplay: $13.00. Eureka! We felt like we had struck it rich; we were on our way!

Then on a gray winter day—Wednesday, January 20, 1988—things in my world started to change. I was sitting in my office at the AT&T Lexington Road plant, when word came down the chain of command that all employees needed to gather in the cafeteria. I thought, *this cannot be good news*. With over 2,000 employees working the day shift, it was standing room only in the cafeteria.

"I received a phone call this morning from AT&T corporate," Ken Raschke, the vice -president for manufacturing and plant manager, started speaking. "AT&T corporate has decided to close the Winston-Salem plant," he continued. The silent crowd turned to gasps and weeping.

In an instant, all 3,300 employees had three options: retire, relocate to other AT&T facilities around the country, or be laid off over the period of the next year. Reactions ranged from disbelief to anger to sorrow.

Only recently, our factory had been recognized for our tremendous strides in improving efficiencies and productivity. No matter. The handwriting was on the wall—manufacturing jobs all over the country were moving overseas, where cheap labor would replace so many of our positions.

While I was deeply saddened for my fellow employees, I had a different, unspoken reaction from anyone else in that room. For months, I'd already been looking at potential AT&T jobs in Washington, DC, so I could be closer to Linda—instead of seeing her on weekends only. Up until this point, my boss had blocked my transfer. But suddenly, overnight, my transfer miraculously got approved.

This was evidence to me, yet again, of God's ultimate reign in our lives. What I could not make happen on my own accord, He orchestrated for me. I would get to work close to my wife, so we would no longer need our late-night phone calls!

I became the first transferee out of Lexington Road. I accepted a job in Bethesda, Maryland, in marketing and sales for AT&T Network Systems. Life may have thrown me a curveball, but God put me in the right position to hit it! This event would go down as one of my defining moments.

This was evidence to me, yet again, of God's ultimate reign in our lives.

In April 1988, Linda and I moved into a newly built home, much like the one we had in North Carolina. We were truly blessed! I often wondered what I'd done to deserve so much, yet I also knew we served a generous God.

AT&T was my job, one that I always loved and appreciated; but the process of relocating to Maryland, complete with weeks of packing and unpacking boxes, proved a major distraction from my music. Once life settled down to a more normal routine with my new job and our new house mostly in order, I was able to get back to the music business—and "Rachel's Song" fan mail—in the evening hours and weekends.

So within a couple of months, I wrote four new songs! Thanks to my experience recording "Rachel's Song," I knew what I needed to do—*get them recorded.*

Recording the Rachel's Song *Album*

I now had seven original songs—three already recorded and four new ones that I had written. I decided that seven was enough to compile an album.

I was eager to have my music on a high-quality CD and cassette tape that could be mass produced. This seemed to align with our goal of helping more people hear the song. CDs were a relatively new format, however—so new that I did not yet own a CD player!

I called Gary Prim.

"Hey Gary," I said excitedly, "I have written four more songs. I wonder if you're up for arranging and recording these for me."

I didn't have to ask twice.

"Fantastic!" he said. "You know the drill, Dave. Send me the lead sheets and a recording of the songs, and I'll start arranging them as soon as I get them!"

Gary and I decided to use Reflections studio again for the recordings, and we would again have Ronny Light as the recording engineer. I felt like I already knew the drill, and I was excited to go back in the studio!

I booked Studio A for Saturday, April 9, 1988. Gene Lawson, the studio owner, again confirmed that he would have the piano freshly tuned for our sessions.

I arrived early at the studio—entering the front door and walking to the left to Studio A. Ronny was already setting up for the day.

After Gary arrived, since he'd already created his arrangements for the music, he played some of the first arrangement of the day for me, starting on the grand piano as he always did—to give me a taste of how the recording would sound.

"Wow, Gary," I told him. "You have outdone yourself once again!"

"Thank you, Dave," Gary replied. "I think I'm ready to do this!" Then, turning towards the control room, he told Ronny, "Let's try recording this first song, if you're ready."

"Got it," Ronny said through the control room mic to the studio. "And we're rollin'."

I had given this piece the working title of "Reflections." Gary nailed it on the first take. We didn't need a second take. *What a professional*, I said to myself.

As Gary did with all the music he arranged for me, he then added multiple layers using his synthesizer.

In less than an hour, recording number one was "in the can," as they say.

Next, Gary played through a song I'd written named "Abundant Joy."

Boom! Gary was a "one-take wonder!" Another song complete.

By now, it was lunchtime. Ronny let me know that the two loves of his life were *recording music*—and *food!*

"Hey," Ronny said enthusiastically, "What do you say we go to the Green Hills Grill?

The three of us piled into my rental car and found a booth in the packed, popular eatery. *Yes sir*, I thought, *always trust the locals when it comes to restaurant recommendations.*

This would become one of our favorite places each time I returned to Nashville—but the food wasn't the only enticement that day. Gary and Ronny knew everyone in the music industry, and I'd get my first experience riding sidecar on one of their celebrity encounters.

"Is that Reba McIntire?" I asked with wide-eyes as a I spotted a pretty, familiar-looking face walking in the front door.

"Yup," Ronny said, hardly looking up. "And if you look at that table over there, that's Ricky Skaggs."

I'd learned that Nashville musicians are like one big, friendly family. What impressed me the most about these famous musicians was how friendly they were and how deferential they were to Gary and Ronny. While music lovers know famous singer/songwriters by sight, Gary and Ronny served as the talent behind the talent. *How amazing is this that I am working with the people behind country music royalty!* I thought, as a new level of gratitude entered my soul. Thinking back to my days playing hymns on the ship for the Honduran orange shippers, I couldn't help but think my daddy would have gotten a kick out of where my music had taken me. And I hoped he would be proud.

The glory wasn't mine, of course, but God's. And I was grateful.

After a memorable lunch experience, we headed back to the studio to record the last two songs, "Wonder of Life" and "Tranquil Moments."

Thanks to Gary's and Ronny's many years of experience, they made this process look easy. By the end of the day, I had four newly recorded songs! As I listened to the final cut of the last song, I considered how all my late-night brainstorming with Linda by phone was coming to fruition, as my music was expanding.

Even More Music!

Even though United Artists had turned down "Danger in Your Love" for the James Bond movie, I really loved the song and wanted to use an instrumental-only version of the recording on my new album. But my only stereo master included the vocals. I would need to convert that recording to instrumental by replacing the vocal tracks with my instrumental melody tracks.

In the summer of 1988, I found Omega Recording Studios in Rockville, Maryland, located just fifteen minutes from my AT&T office in Bethesda. When I called the owner, Bob Yesbek, and told him what

I needed, he assured me he could help. I booked the studio time on a Saturday, so Linda could again be part of the studio experience—and brought my Yamaha DX-7 synthesizer (just like the one Gary Prim had) and master 2-inch tape.

This was a different studio than I'd ever recorded in, but I had become more familiar with the process. After Bob set up everything, I put on the headphones so I could hear the other instruments. We rolled tape, and I played the melody using the distinctive electric piano sound on the Yamaha DX-7—the same sound that Gary Prim had used on "Rachel's Song."

I wasn't quite as skilled as Gary, but after re-recording a few spots (recording engineers call these *punch-ins*) to tighten up my timing, I liked the results. Bob carefully mixed the recording down to stereo and made me a master tape and couple of cassette tapes. That same day, we walked out with our new instrumental song, which I renamed simply, "Your Love."

As we walked out of Omega Recording Studios, I looked at Linda and said, "Now that I have seven songs recorded, what do I do next?"

To help me answer that question, I immediately knew I'd need some advice from Ronny in Nashville.

CHAPTER NINE

CUSTOMERS ARE THE BEST MUSIC AMBASSADORS

*"['Rachel's Song']…is so fresh, vital—yet relaxing—and full
of love and warmth."*
~ANN

Lessons in Mass Production

"Hey, Ronny," I greeted him over the phone. "I have my seven songs ready to put on an album. But I don't know the next step. What do I need to make that a reality?"

"I'll tell you what," he said. "Let me introduce you to Randy Kling at DiscMastering. If you want the best sound quality, he's your guy. He has done work for the biggest stars in Nashville, and he can do it for you. Your album will sound as good as any other album in Nashville."

God was expanding His orchestra, yet again! I was excited to meet yet another key player.

I really liked Randy. When I visited him, he took me on a tour of his facility.

"And in this studio over here," he said, pointing to an empty studio, "I worked with Elvis Presley."

Wow! Talk about music royalty! I was becoming less surprised by these brushes with celebrity, but hearing about legends who'd walked my same paths never stopped leaving me feeling *honored.*

Randy told me all about what his mastering process involved.

"Have you ever noticed that television commercials seem louder than the actual shows?" he asked. "That's on purpose. It's how the commercials are mastered. Producers want them to be louder, so you can't ignore them even when you go into the kitchen to grab a snack! Well, what we do here is to make sure that doesn't happen with your recording. We want each song on the album to have a similar volume and texture."

Since I had only seven songs, and a cassette tape would hold an hour's worth of music, I decided to put all seven songs on one side, and the same seven songs on the backside (or B-Side as they call it)! And for the CD—well, I still didn't own a CD player, so I didn't know about the CD player's automatic repeat function. I decided to put my seven songs on the CD twice—just as I had done for the cassette. While I did this as a pragmatic solution to extend the length of my album (and out of naïveté), it turned out to be a blessing in disguise. Every time the cassette or CD got played, the songs were played twice. Without knowing it, having songs play a second time made them feel more familiar, and people got to enjoy them twice! I like to think God was behind my naïve decision!

For every subsequent album that I produced after "Rachel's Song," I had it mastered by Randy Kling or his son, Chad, at DiscMastering. As a footnote, Randy received a Lifetime Achievement Award in the field of audio engineering at the Country Music Hall of Fame and Museum on June 7, 2015, in Nashville. You can find a wonderful article about Randy in the June 15, 2015, edition of the *Tennessean* newspaper. Look for the title, "Gallatin Man Mastered Sound for the Stars."

Getting "Rachel's Song" Cassettes and CDs Mass Produced

In 1988, only fifty CD manufacturers existed worldwide. One of the best CD manufacturers in the US was called Technetronics in West Chester, Pennsylvania. I always wanted to know the people I did business with, so I called to arrange a time for a personal tour of their facility. Linda and I drove up to Pennsylvania. As we walked through their facility, I found that their use of robotics enabled an almost completely automated process.

"This is the wave of the future," I whispered to Linda.

We watched the machines churn out Michael Jackson's *Bad* CD. His sales were so big that nearly all CD manufacturing capacity in the country had been committed to manufacturing that one album!

Satisfied that Technetronics could certainly meet our needs, I started designing the cover artwork for the "Rachel's Song" CD and cassette as soon as we got home. I found a beautiful photo that I had taken of a pink dogwood in our yard, which I decided would make the ideal centerpiece of the cassette and CD cover. By the middle of August, I placed my order for 500 CDs.

I also ordered 1,000 cassettes from a separate Nashville company—Custom Tape Duplicators, the premier facility at the time, owned by the Tant family. When the CDs were delivered to our home in Maryland, it felt like Christmas when I unwrapped them. I held a shiny case in my hand, thinking, *this technology is no longer the future; it's my present!*

With a basement full of CDs and cassettes of my complete album, I was positioned for growth. After hearing my music on the radio all over the country, fans kept ordering my music and writing me letters of appreciation. Everyone who heard "Rachel's Song" kept asking, "When are you going to have more music available?" Finally, all the ingredients for success were within reach—a quality product, and a growing and eager fan base wanting my music.

This is it, I told myself. *I can begin to see a path to success with my music.* Honestly, I could not have dreamed that the pieces would fall into place as they had.

Then another thought popped into my head.

Learning What NOT to Do

What on earth do I do next to expand my library of music? Maybe I should repeat what I did in Winston-Salem when I first wrote Rachel's Song—seek help from a local songwriters' association.

I started looking for a local songwriters' association in Maryland affiliated with the Nashville Songwriters Association. I quickly found the Songwriters Association of Washington (SAW), and I attended one of their evening meetings.

When I walked into that fire station in downtown Georgetown, Washington, DC, I met the friendliest folks—most of them walking around with their guitars in their left hand as they mingled about chatting with friends. Once the meeting started, a member led a songwriting discussion. We sat there in our folding chairs in a small conference room, hoping to find a formula for success with our music. Then, one by one, any member that had a new song was invited to play and sing it for the group's critique. Some songs were good—and some not so much. Comments were generally expressed in a kind but straightforward and honest tone.

I enjoyed the meeting, but I felt like my instrumental music didn't fit into the interests of this group.

But just because this meeting didn't offer me any big insights, it did lead me to a big opportunity. I learned that the Washington Area Musicians Association (WAMA) convention would be held in a few weeks. The all-day event featured representatives from every aspect of the music business.

"Isn't God good?" I exclaimed to Linda when I got home. "He led me to the songwriting association, so I could learn about the convention coming up. Isn't it great the way things work out?"

Surely, the convention would open doors and give me some useful information. And it was always a good thing to meet people in the industry who could nudge me in the right direction.

I drove to the convention that Saturday morning, toting a few promo packages of my music—including my CD of "Rachel's Song." Even before the 10:00 a.m. opening, the place already looked packed.

This convention is a bigger deal than I had imagined, I thought as I reviewed the list of speakers and panelists: BMI, ASCAP, the Copyright Office, big-name music publishers, major record store chains, artist representatives, as well as some well-known songwriters.

I attended both the large and smaller break-out sessions. One topic really spoke to my interest: "How to Sell to Record Stores." After the panelists spoke, they opened the floor to questions from participants.

I spoke up quickly. "I have a question about my instrumental music recording...." I went on to describe the genre as soothing, relaxing, instrumental piano music that had been played on easy-listening radio stations across the globe. "So, what I want to know is, how do I get this into more record stores?"

The three panelists looked at one another, blinked a few times, then looked back at me.

"Um, instrumental?" one of them asked. "Do you mean like elevator music?"

I quickly learned that none of them had any idea what to do with instrumental music! I shook it off. *Not in their wheelhouse, I guess!*

I participated in several other sessions throughout the day, and I asked the same question. No panelist could answer my question! But a funny thing happened. I started to generate "groupies," a bunch of people who followed me from session to session, just to hear me get shot down by the so-called music "experts." I chuckled to myself as they cheered me on, but I still had no answer.

How can it be this hard? I wondered. *I had more luck looking for radio towers for radio stations to play my music than getting copies of these recordings into the hands of fans through record stores!*

I had one hope left. The conference set aside one hour with experts scattered around the perimeter of the ballroom. During that hour, participants could pick these professionals' brains.

I made a beeline to the table for Record Bar, one of the largest music retail chains in the country. I did a little dance of anticipation, as I got in line to talk to someone from the place I had tried unsuccessfully for months to introduce to "Rachel's Song." Ironically, Record Bar's headquarters were in Durham, North Carolina, just down the road from Winston-Salem.

When I reached the front of the line, I told the young "expert" the same thing I'd shared in each breakout session. While I talked, I saw my groupies piling up behind and around me, crowding in to hear the answer from the expert.

When I finished my pitch, I reached out with a copy of my "promotional package" to hand to the expert. Before my hand even got within his reach, he held up the universal "stop" gesture, then actually pushed the package back at me.

"No need to give me that," he said with a flat expression. "Instrumental music doesn't sell. Sorry, I can't help you."

"Thank you for your time," I said. "Here, I'd like you to have a copy just the same…Keep this to remind you, someday, that you turned down a successful recording."

The groupies around me exploded into applause.

After the long day—and a forty-five-minute drive home—I played the events of the day over in my mind. *Why didn't any of these music professionals understand my music? Don't they put any value at all on the quality or appeal of music? Everyone who has heard this music wants to buy a copy of it. Do these people not want to make money? Or is their musical taste so different that they just don't get it?*

When I got home, Linda greeted me while making dinner.

"How did it go?" she asked cheerfully.

"I don't know what I'm going to do with my music," I said, slamming my bag of materials onto the kitchen counter. "But I'll tell you what I'm not going to do. I'm not having anything to do with those people. They have no clue what to do with my kind of music!"

Until I opened my mouth, I didn't realize how the events of the day had gotten under my skin. I'd shaken off the first panelist's snub—assuming he was the outlier. When his rhetoric was repeated by every "expert" in that convention, it left me doubting—the *experts* mostly, but in some small way, doubting *myself*.

Had I made a mistake, printing so many copies of a CD that, until I bought my first CD player, I couldn't even play myself?

As Linda hugged me, she said in her understanding, comforting tone, "I know there's a way. We just have to keep working to find it."

I learned a valuable life lesson that day. Sometimes, you learn what to do from experts; other times, they teach you a more important lesson, like what *not* to do.

Never being one to wallow for long in my defeat, as I got ready for bed that night, I looked in the mirror, closed my eyes, and said a little prayer. "Dear Lord. I know this is *not it*, so please show me what *it is* that I'm supposed to do."

And then I waited for Him to shed His light on the subject.

I didn't have long to wait.

When Music Speaks to Your Heart, It Stops You in Your Tracks

I felt blessed to work with my new AT&T family in Maryland. Not only did I love the work, but I enjoyed my team as well. I cannot credit my manager, Tom Abbott, enough for the culture he created—one that was both supportive and productive. In addition to making the environment so positive, Tom and my own immediate boss, Dick McFaul, were supportive of my outside interest in music. What a bonus!

Leslie, a team member of mine whose desk sat directly behind me, asked me a favor.

"Hey, Dave," she said. "I was thinking. A friend of mine owns a gift shop called America in Old Town Alexandria, Virginia. Do you think it would be okay if I gave her a CD of 'Rachel's Song'? I think she'd love it."

"Well, of course, Leslie," I answered. "Here, let me give you a copy to share with your friend."

I didn't think much more about that exchange until a few days later when Leslie came into work with some news.

"Hey, Dave," Leslie greeted me.

"Hi, Leslie. How are you this beautiful morning?" I asked.

"I'm great," she said with a smile. "Hey, do you remember my friend, Jane? She's the one I gave a copy of your music to. Well, she called me last night. She told me that she'd love to talk with you about your music. She loved it! And her customers love it. That's what she wants to talk with you about."

A few evenings later, I picked Linda up from work in downtown DC, and after a nice dinner with my bride in Old Town Alexandria, we visited Jane in her store on King Street, right in the heart of Old Town.

From the sound system in her store, patriotic music reached our ears.

When Linda and I first entered Jane's shop—simply named, America—we were greeted with an attractive boutique devoted to patriotic and Americana merchandise. From the sound system in her store, patriotic music reached our ears.

"You must be Jane," I said as I extended my hand. After making a full round of introductions, she gave us a tour.

"Let me show you something," Jane said with anticipation as she walked us over to her multi-CD player.

"When Leslie gave me your CD, I added it to the CD carousel," she explained. "I play the CDs on a random setting, where it plays one song from each CD until it's played through them all. Anyway, whenever a tune from your CD plays, the customers stop in their tracks!"

"Really?" I asked. "So, they like it?"

"They *love* it!" she corrected me. "Whoever is in the store usually comes to the counter to ask me what music I'm playing. And then they ask me if I sell copies. Do you know what I tell them?" Jane said with a smile in her eyes. "I say, 'Not yet. But I'm going to very soon.' And that's why I wanted to meet you."

Jane clearly was a very astute, enterprising businesswoman—quick to recognize an opportunity.

"Now, will you sell me some CDs and cassettes at a wholesale price for me to play and sell in my shop?"

"Of course!" I responded with gusto. "Let's settle on a price, and then I'll get your order ready tonight!" God was answering our prayers about what to do with all those CDs I'd amassed in our new home! I'd secured reinforcement that there would be a place for them—and that they would touch even more people.

That night, I gathered up her order and hand-delivered it the next day.

I was more than a little surprised when she called me a few days later.

"Well, Dave, all of those tapes and CDs you brought me are sold out," she started off telling me. "Nearly every customer in my shop that hears your music wants to take it home with them. How quickly can you bring me some more?" she asked.

"I will bring you some tonight after work," I told her enthusiastically.

Our relationship with Jane started a new tradition for Linda and me. Each week, Linda and I would meet for a lovely dinner in Old Town, and then we'd head over to see Jane at America to drop off a new shipment of music.

Jane wasn't the only one with enterprising ideas. My thoughts quickly returned to the concept of compound interest and duplication. Let's see, *if I make X dollars with one gift shop, the music could earn 5X dollars if I had five gift shops. And what if I had just one gift shop in each state? Well, that would be 50X dollars! How about five in each state? 250X dollars!* Looking at how much income was being generated from just this one shop, I realized, *now we're talkin' some real income to support my music endeavors.* More importantly, it would mean touching thousands more lives with soft, soothing music.

For years, Linda and I had talked about how to reach more listeners and customers. She and I had talked, brainstormed, and researched, hoping that it would dawn on us. *Could this be THE IT—that moment that could launch our music to another level of success?* we wondered. For us, any success we had with selling our music meant two things: First, others were being touched by the songs I'd worked hard to create and distribute. And second, I could justify and support pouring more energy (and money) into expanding that music.

Our journey to this decisive point had taken us through many defining and threshold moments.

Defining moments—like the Winston-Salem AT&T manufacturing plant closing and Linda's job offer in DC, which brought us to Maryland. Neither of us saw those events coming. They seemed to just happen, as part of life.

Then there was the Washington Area Musicians Association convention, where I experienced a threshold moment when the "music expert" dismissed my instrumental music—without even listening to it! At that point, I could either *give up*, or *push on*. I chose the latter.

But when I lined up all the pieces—from moving to Maryland with AT&T, to writing and recording an entire album of music, to pressing on after rejection, to co-worker Leslie just happening to know a friend with a gift shop—an ah-ha moment formed. It was as if all the seemingly unrelated portions of my life were being sewn together, to reveal a magnificent garment. I could finally see how everything related—and why those events had happened.

And what happened next further cemented in my heart and mind that these events were all part of God's design.

CHAPTER TEN

Juggling Two "Jobs"

"If it were not for beautiful music, I could not go on.
It is much more than entertainment."
~MELLIE

Another Godwink

A short time later, sometime in 1988, another AT&T team member, Jerry Hughes, and I were having lunch and I told him about how well my music had sold in Alexandria. He told me about the town he lived in: Ellicott City, Maryland.

"It's a perfect spot to sell your music," Jerry said. "It's a tourist town, full of gift shops. Why don't you come visit and try to find other shops that will carry your music?"

The next weekend, Linda and I drove to Ellicott City on a bright Saturday morning. Walking into a gift shop called Discoveries on the quaint and popular Main Street, we saw a horde of customers milling about. I perked up my ears. Sure enough, instrumental music played over the sound system.

"Good morning, ma'am," I said to the woman behind the counter. "I wonder if the owner of the shop happens to be in today?"

"You found me," she responded. "I'm Sally Fox. How can I help you?"

"Let me introduce you to my wife—and myself," I said as I made a round of introductions. "I just want to say what a beautiful shop you have here...and we just *love* the music you're playing."

"Well, thank you," she returned.

"I wonder if you'd be willing to listen to some new music," I asked Sally.

"Sure," she said. "Do you have it with you?"

"Yes, I have it right here." I handed her a cassette tape.

Unexpectedly, Sally immediately popped it into her cassette player. As soon as the first notes of "Rachel's Song" played, I witnessed what Jane had told me happened in her store. It was as if a gentle, soothing wave flowed through the shop, stopping everyone in their tracks. People stood still and listened—absorbing the sweet sound. Then several customers came to the counter where Linda and I stood with Sally.

I might not have believed the customers' response to the music had I not seen it myself.

"What are you playing now? Do you have it for sale?" they asked Sally.

I might not have believed the customers' response to the music had I not seen it myself.

Without skipping a beat, Sally looked at me and asked, "How many do you have with you?" Another savvy businesswoman!

I shifted into fulfillment mode and headed back to the car to check on the stock I had brought with us that day. I could have kicked myself when I opened the trunk to find that I only had six cassettes with me! I sold them to Sally at wholesale on the spot.

But those six didn't meet Sally's immediate problem. I watched her customers rush to the front counter, jockeying to buy one of those six copies.

I sent her a larger order as soon as I got back home that day—which wouldn't be the last. Sally became one of our highly valued customers.

In moments like this, I felt like God was looking down at me with a smile—and a wink—letting me know I was doing the work He'd ordained.

Introducing "Rachel's Song" on Foot

After witnessing firsthand the music being played at the Discoveries shop—and then snatched off the counter by customers hungry for its inspiration—I knew my sales model for the CDs and cassettes was working. Just like the music could be duplicated onto those simple devices, I knew my model for distribution could be duplicated—if I worked at it!

On weekends, I learned about the local markets and gift shops. Before long, I had more than twenty gift shops selling my music. Each day after work, my answering machine was full of gift shop owners placing additional orders for my music. I never tired of coming home after a long day to my second job of packing up new orders. On my way to work the next morning, I'd take them to PKG's packaging store for shipment.

My work regularly took me to Philadelphia by Amtrak from Washington, DC—*exposing me to more markets!* On my way to my boarding gate to catch the train, like everyone else, I'd walk through the beautiful, historic Union Station grand entrance hall. On one trip, I got to Union Station a little early and window shopped in the many little stores around the entrance hall. My eye caught a gift shop named Reunion Brass Gallery, a place selling high-quality, expertly displayed, Williamsburg brass gifts and accessories. I popped in as my ears were greeted with beautiful classical music playing on their high-end Bose music system.

I approached the owner of the shop, Kathy Loots, and complimented her on the beautiful-sounding music. I asked her about possibly playing and selling my music, and I gave her a CD of "Rachel's Song" to play.

"We don't sell music," Kathy told me. "We only sell brass items."

Not to be deterred, every time I returned to Union Station, I stopped in Reunion Brass Gallery—and again asked Kathy about selling my music.

For over six months, Kathy told me the same thing. "We love your music, but we are a brass shop. *We don't sell music.*"

"Well, let me ask you a question," I tried another approach. "Do people ask you about the music you play in your shop?"

"Oh, yes. A lot of people ask about it," she responded. "But we aren't a music shop."

Kathy couldn't seem to see the connection between my music and her customers. Here they stood—attracted to my music, interested in purchasing it, and ready to hand her money, if only she had the music available for sale. I wondered to myself: *Had Kathy and Jim forgotten why they owned a business in the first place? To make their customers happy— and make money!*

I consider myself to be both patient and persistent. The heart of business is the relationship between supplier and merchant—as well as between merchant and customer. Relationships happen over time, not on command. So, I took my time with Kathy, just as I had done with so many other relationships in my life. I didn't ever pressure her— despite wondering why she didn't want to make money selling a CD her customers clearly wanted!

On another trip, Kathy's husband, Jim, was working behind the counter. Once again, I tried to nudge the door open by asking him about selling my music.

"As we've told you before, Dave..." Jim repeated.

Here it comes again, I thought, smiling warmly as I always do, yet anticipating their rejection.

"We love your music, but we sell brass items. Music doesn't fit into our business model."

"Well, how about this," I tried with one more push. "You see that lovely Williamsburg bowl over there by your cash register? Why don't you put some of my cassettes and CDs in that bowl, and when someone asks about them, see what happens? I mean, they won't take up any of your shelf or floor space, right?"

Reluctantly, Jim glanced at the bowl, undoubtedly seeing that he had the room to stock those few products. Skeptically, he agreed to give it a try. Judging from the look in his eyes, I think he acquiesced just to keep me from asking again!

When I stopped by a few days later as I passed through town, Kathy and Jim greeted me a little differently.

"Well, when you're right, you're right," Jim laughed. "And I'll be the first to admit that you, Dave, were right about the cassettes and CDs. We sold out the same day you left them here!"

Amazingly, they became a wonderful customer, and over the next year, they sold over $35,000 (at wholesale) of my one-and-only (at the time) CD of *Rachel's Song*!

Not only that, but Jim and Kathy started playing *only* my music in their shop— continuously, for twelve hours each day. Kathy told me that neither she and her husband, nor their staff, ever got tired of listening to those seven songs on the *Rachel's Song* CD, even though they played it all day long. I considered that a really high compliment.

Jim and Kathy used a sophisticated point-of-sale system. By tracking every item in their store and the square footage of space it occupied, they quickly discovered a new leader in sales per square foot. The *Rachel's Song* CD beat every other item in the store! They made thousands of dollars each year, without using up much space at all—just a simple display by the cash register.

Jim and Kathy loved to laugh and tell the story of how long it had taken them to realize what they were missing, once they learned they could play and sell music so successfully in their brass shop. It was time to expand on that success....

As I continued to physically visit prospective gift shops to find customers, I noticed many of them played music from the Midwest and West Coast—artists like Ray Lynch and Jonathon Lee. I reached out to Jonathon Lee, famous for his outdoor performances in Big Sur, California. I learned that we both had the same goal of securing gift shop customers to play and sell our respective albums of music.

"Here's what I propose, Jonathon," I said. "How about we exchange customers? I'll send you my top twenty customers on the East Coast, if you send me your top twenty customers on the West Coast."

He agreed, and we each exchanged twenty customers. I wish I could have offered to exchange more, but at the time I only had twenty customers!

Once again, God was orchestrating. Overnight, after I set up distribution to those customers, my business virtually doubled!

Cold-Calling "Rachel's Song"

About the time I reached forty customers, I realized that I couldn't keep working my strategy of going from town to town and store to store every weekend to find those willing to sell my music. We were running out of towns within driving distance, which also had enough gift shops.

"Why don't you start prospecting for new customers by telephone?" Linda suggested. "This could really expand your reach and cut down our driving."

Business is a relationship, and I liked to build relationships face-to-face. To me, part of the joy—and connection—was seeing the shop manager's smile when they heard my music, witnessing customers interacting with the merchandise, and mentally picturing the store during each subsequent interaction and sale.

Besides, when I was in the store, I knew I had a lot more control over the situation than I did on a phone line.

"I'm not sure that would work," I countered. "When you're face-to-face with a customer, they can't hang up on you. My music and business style are personal, so I think I need to physically meet with people to make a sale."

Fortunately, Linda had made a good point—and like I had done with Jim and Kathy when I knew they could sell my music if they simply put it on display, she didn't let up. In fact, she continued bringing it up until she convinced me to give it a try!

Now I needed a list of lots of gift shops—and their phone numbers.

In those pre-Google days, I visited the Library of Congress one evening after work. I found the phone book room, where I made photocopies of the yellow pages for gift shops in several major US cities. Once I had my lists, I used my Saturdays to make phone calls. It wasn't quite the same as driving around the country and meeting folks face to face, but it did save time—and gas!

"Do you sell any cassette tapes of the music you play in your shop?" I said as part of the script I developed and used on each call.

If they said "no," I simply said "thank you" and hung up.

If they said "no, but we play music," then I would ask them if they would consider selling the music. If so, I would get their mailing information and send them a free sample.

The third response I occasionally got was a flat-out "yes." In that case, I also asked if I could send them my music to consider.

The hardest part was getting used to hearing "no." A lot!

The shop owners that played and sold the music they played never said "no." Who could say "no" to receiving free music?

I can't say this process was easy. For every thirty gift shops I called, I only got one yes to send a free sample. The hardest part was getting used to hearing "no." A lot! And I felt it was easier to say no over the phone than it had been face to face. What kept me going was the occasional "yes."

As a funny sidenote, at that time, our phone bill from AT&T came itemized—listing each call, regardless of length. I made so many calls each month that our phone bill started being sent to us in a box the size of a shoebox! Twenty-nine out of thirty phone calls were only thirteen seconds long—those were the no's.

After doing this for several weekends, I decided there had to be a better way—a more efficient way to find customers. Trips to the Library of Congress to make copies of yellow page listings were time-consuming. After a bit of research, I learned that I could purchase a list of all the gift shops in the United States, alphabetically by town and state. It wasn't cheap, but I ordered the printout anyway.

When it came, my eyes bugged out of my head. The list was a 4-inch-thick computer printout on wide computer paper—*45,000 gift shops!*

It shouldn't take me more than a couple of decades to call through this list, I thought to myself. But if I could target the stores that might be interested, I would have a much smaller list.

I quickly learned that calls to gift shops in major cities were a waste of time. I had much more success with tourist towns—like Ellicott City, Maryland; Blowing Rock, North Carolina; and Gatlinburg, Tennessee. I knew those towns had tons of gift shops and a small, permanent population. That meant they had a constant influx of new customers.

I needed a way to find towns just like those.

One day on my lunch hour, I visited the local library, conveniently located just across the street from my office. There I found a huge book called the *Rand McNally Commercial Atlas and Marketing Guide of the US.*

Wow! This is the gold mine I've been looking for! I thought.

When I got home that day, I ordered my own copy of it for about one hundred dollars.

The book was huge—15 x 21 x 1.5 inches—and weighed twelve pounds, as much as a bowling ball. But this made quick work of what I needed for my own data analytics. Remember, those were the days before data analytics even existed as a recognized discipline! Using the list I had purchased, for each town, I counted the number of gift shops and looked up its population in the atlas. I entered the name of the town, state, number of gift shops, and population into a database I created on my Apple computer. Then I had the computer calculate the ratio of population-per-gift-shop in each town. Sorting this database by this ratio allowed me to find towns in each state with the lowest ratio of population-per-gift-shop—in other words, the most gift shops per resident. Low and behold, Gatlinburg, Blowing Rock, Ellicott City, rose to the top of the list—like cream rises to the top of fresh whole milk! I was onto something....

Ah-ha! Now, instead of shooting in the dark—or making blind calls—I could prioritize my call list, focusing on the small tourist towns across the entire country. This had to go down as one of my biggest ah-ha moments ever. I felt blessed to have the computer skills to target the stores I knew would love my music.

Picking up the phone, I said a short prayer before dialing the first number on my list. I was using the same script as before, but this time, I would apply my homegrown data analytics. *Would it make a difference?* I wondered as the first call connected.

The short, happy answer was a big YES!

My success rate went from one in thirty—to one in five! Every weekend, I worked that phone from morning until night, and by the time each Saturday business day ended, my voice was giving out. But because of the work I put in that day, I had accumulated fifty to seventy-five prospective gift shops wanting a sample cassette tape or CD of my music.

You know you are in the right line of work when you cannot wait to get back to it. I felt doubly blessed since I not only loved my day-job, but I also loved my after-hours music business. In fact, I could not wait until Saturday morning to start making calls to find new gift shop customers!

Some people would cringe at having to do sales calls—especially on their day off. Not me! I could just envision all those tourists in small towns throughout the United States walking into gift shops and being so taken by the soothing, relaxing, beautiful music that they wanted to take it home with them. And, based upon past experience, besides connecting with the purchasers in the gift shops, I would soon hear from many of their customers—as they would tell me their stories of how they first heard the music and how it touched them. (You will hear more about those stories soon!)

CHAPTER ELEVEN

I WONDER WHAT COMES NEXT?

"I've never been touched by music quite like this before. This is the most relaxing, sensual, yet powerful music I've ever heard. I can't stop listening."
~JENNIFER

L inda's strategy was working. After a few weeks of making phone calls instead of personal visits like I had been doing, I came home daily to an answering machine full of messages from customers—placing new orders.

Remember what I said about musicians needing more than mere talent to succeed? I loved creating music; but I also loved it when my music touched people—and *more* people! I'd work for AT&T each day, giving them my all. Then I'd spend each evening creating gift shop invoices and packing orders.

Expanding my reach meant working very hard.

As a result, I leaped from forty gift shops on both coasts— to over a thousand outlets all around the United States.

Fan mail continued pouring in, bringing my vision of *happy* customers touched by the music into focus. Many of them encouraged me to write more music—and record another album.

The question was, *how do I find the time?*

My First Christmas Album

My two jobs kept me so busy that I hadn't taken the time to compose new music. It dawned on me that instead of writing new music for my next album, perhaps I could create a Christmas album of my favorite Christmas carols.

"Gary," I said to my now-dear friend over the phone, "I want to do a Christmas album. I could sure use your help."

"I'd love to work with you again, Dave," Gary said cheerfully. "By now, you know what to do. Send me what you've got, and let me know when you want to book some studio time."

I sent Gary my twelve favorite Christmas carols. Then I added a couple of special songs.

First, I included a copy of a song I wrote called "Happy Christmas Bells."

Then, I added one my father, Joe Combs, had written called "King of Kings Is Born." As I added his song to my list, I paused, appreciating the moment. I reminisced at all the devotion my daddy had given me—playing hymns that fed my love of, and success with, music. I felt that God was allowing me to connect with Daddy in a small yet profound way. My father hadn't sold his music or had nearly the success I'd already had, yet he loved music every bit as much as I did. *This one's for you, Daddy*, I thought, finalizing my list for Gary.

I reconnected with my favorite recording engineer, Ronny Light, and booked Reflections recording studio yet again—for the summer of 1989. At first, it felt a bit strange to play and record Christmas music in the heat of summer! But I warmed up to it, pun intended. Gary did his wonderful job of arranging and performing these Christmas songs. After listening to the master recording of my second music album, I knew we had another winner.

Once I got back home to Maryland, I worked on cover artwork for the new album, which I titled, *First Christmas*. I wanted to use one of my own photos to make the cover more personal instead of just purchasing stock photography. Since it was summer, that meant getting a photo with snow was out of the question!

"Hey, Linda," I said to my wife, "What do you think about a photo of the corn-shuck doll Christmas ornament that we hang on our Christmas tree every year?"

"I think that's it, Dave," she agreed. "And what if you hang it in one of those tall, long-needle pine trees in our neighborhood that we love so much?"

We took the corn-shuck ornament out of Christmas storage. Later that morning, we visited the pine tree with camera in hand.

"Perfect," I said after snapping the photo. This might seem like an insignificant detail—and a part of the story I could have omitted. But it's meaningful for two reasons.

First, that ornament holds a special place in our hearts, reminding us of my Grandmother Combs, my Aunt Phyllis Combs, and my father—all of whom were very skilled at making dolls and other items out of corn shucks. I was honoring my lineage—and carrying forward their creative legacy.

Second, I was reminded that I didn't need great riches or resources to create something marvelous. When God oversaw the orchestra of my life, He became the master composer—letting my stress over the details vanish. This "homegrown" cover became evidence that He'd always place *the right note at just the right time* in His masterpiece score.

I released "First Christmas" in September of 1989. I sent an announcement to every fan who had written to me about my past music, as well as all the shops that had carried my first album. Orders poured in from fans and store managers/purchasers who received the mailing. Distributors were also happy to have some new music from Combs Music!

God Grows Combs Music Within Our Walls

God's orchestra was playing in full force—and had not yet reached the crescendo!

1990 was a year of tremendous growth for Combs Music, both with orders from nationwide fans and gift shops. There weren't enough hours in the day to handle my full-time job at AT&T and continue giving excellent customer service to my Combs Music customers. It was clear that it was time for us to hire a full-time office manager.

While I had hired many people in the corporate world, this was different. I would need sound advice and help in finding the right person for the job.

Our circle of friends just happened to include a wonderful businesswoman in Winston-Salem, Betty Wade, who owned a successful temporary employment agency, Professional Office Personnel Inc.

(POPI). Betty graciously gave me a contact for a Maryland temp agency. When I called and told them what I needed—a full-time office manager who would enjoy working alone in a private home largely unsupervised, and was trustworthy—they were happy to assist.

When they sent Jane Wilkes, I knew quickly that she was the perfect person for the job. She had a wonderful personality, was completely trustworthy, and loved working independently—which was fortunate, since it would just be her and our cat, Melody, working in our finished basement all day while Linda and I were at work! I hired Jane full-time. Her administrative efficiency took a tremendous load off of me, allowing me to concentrate on the creative side of Combs Music.

The BOB Technique and the Beautiful Thoughts *Album*

In January of 1990, I felt that my crucial time creating music had been neglected. With Linda's encouragement, I decided I would begin dedicating an hour a day to sitting at the piano and letting my creative juices flow. I would get up an hour earlier and stay at the piano every day until I had at least the beginnings of a new song. Since Linda was already an early riser—up at 5:00 a.m. and off to work by 6:00 a.m.—it was a simple change to my routine which I hoped would reap a return.

> **I would get up an hour earlier and stay at the piano every day until I had at least the beginnings of a new song.**

Linda lovingly called my special song-writing time and technique—the BOB technique—short for putting my "Behind On the Bench!" (Parents and music teachers, feel free to use this model too!) This worked beautifully, and within a couple of months, I had written thirteen new songs, enough for a new album.

Once I finished those thirteen songs, like clockwork, I sent them to Gary Prim. I expected him to create what I knew would be wonderful arrangements.

Our music-making routine continued. In March of 1990, I booked Gary, Ronny Light the recording engineer, and Reflections recording studio in Nashville for a week. Spending a week in the studio with Gary and Ronny was always such a wonderful and memorable experience. To walk into the studio on Monday morning with nothing but musical notes on a piece of paper, and by Friday to leave with finished recordings of absolutely inspiring music seemed like a miracle to me.

This time was no different.

As Linda, Ronny, and I sat in the studio control room watching through the glass, Gary's hands floated across the keys. As we listened to the captivating sounds, I could almost read Linda's mind through the thoughtful, pleasant expressions that danced across her beautiful face. Even before the song was over, I could see Linda jotting down a phrase that I knew would become the perfect title for each song—titles like "Peaceful Places," "Serene Blue Sky," "Gentle Breezes."

While we were in the studio busily recording, a friend of Ronny's, Johnny Lauffer, dropped in to say hi to Ronny. Ronny introduced Johnny to Linda and me and told us that Johnny was a great piano player in his own right. Johnny was very friendly with a great personality, and we liked him immediately. He told us that he had played piano for Dolly Parton for many years. We invited Johnny to stay with us in the control room and listen as we recorded Gary playing my original songs. Johnny absolutely loved the music he was hearing. I can still see Johnny sitting on the sofa, eyes closed, nodding his head in approval as Gary played, soaking in the music and uttering that universal approval expression— umm, umm, umm! It did my heart good to see him enjoying the music so much. He was so complimentary of Gary's arrangements and performance. Our friendship with Johnny has lasted through the years.

By May, the new cassettes and CDs of the album, *Beautiful Thoughts*, were ready for distribution and sales. Next to the *Rachel's Song* album, *Beautiful Thoughts* is still one of my favorites—not only for its sound and how fun the songs are to play, but because of how it came from those sacred morning hours. I felt it was God's return gift for the time I'd dedicated to expressing His voice through my head and fingers.

St. Louis Concert and The Lettermen

Back home from Nashville, I was greeted by a week's worth of very special letters that our office manager, Jane, had answered and neatly left on my desk for me to read. She said, "Dave, every day your mailbox was filled with these very special letters."

I've shared bits of these letters throughout this book, and I've mentioned my fan mail, but I haven't yet shared the "backstory" of what was happening. People would often write, telling me the story of how they first heard my music—usually on the radio or in gift shops. From those letters (which I will talk more about soon!), I learned that my music was playing in all major markets in the country—usually on easy-listening stations.

Not only was it playing, but it was playing *a lot*. In fact, it hit the charts in major markets—and in smaller markets as well.

One of these radio stations was KEZK-FM in St. Louis. Soon, I received a telephone call from Jim Doyle, the program director.

"Hi Dave," he started off. "Thanks for taking my call. Let me jump in. We held a contest at our radio station asking listeners to tell us the names of their favorite artists. You were one of the top five most requested performers. If you're up for it, I'd love to fly you here to perform at a live concert we're hosting on September 30 at Buder Park, which is a large outdoor venue. We are expecting over 25,000 people to attend."

My mind began picturing a crowd of 25,000 people. I didn't think I'd ever been to a musical event that large—and I knew I hadn't played for one! I thought back to the small crowd on the orange ships in Tampa Bay. A part of me thought, *if only Daddy could hear about how those days playing hymns with him had led to this!*

"Well, that's quite an honor," I said, still a bit shocked. "Do you mind if I ask who the other performers are that you've invited?"

"We have George Benson, The Lettermen, The Association, Don McLean, and you, if you're willing," he told me. "We'll cover all expenses for you and your wife—airfare, limo service, hotel. Everything. It might be a nice way for you to meet your fans and sign autographs too. And of course, I'd love it if you'd bring copies of your music to sell."

I knew a great opportunity when I heard one, and this one seemed almost too good to be true. But I knew it was real, so I wasted no time in responding, "Jim, I would love to take part in your event."

As I waited for the September concert date and went on with my weekly routine of working by day and managing Combs Music by evening and weekend, AT&T business took me to Pittsburgh, where I was having a summer evening dinner by myself at a big upscale restaurant in Union Station. As I frequently do, I struck up a conversation with my waiter about my music. I mentioned the upcoming concert with George Benson, Don McLean, and others.

"What a small world," the waiter said. "George Benson and his family are having dinner right over there," he said, nodding to a table in the back. "You know that he is from Pittsburgh," he said.

I thought to myself, *this is not a coincidence.*

After I finished my meal, I kept glancing over at George to see if he was finished eating. I wanted to talk with him, but I didn't want to interrupt his family time.

Finally, after the server removed their empty dishes from the table, I stood up and walked over to him.

"Hi," I said, "I don't mean to interrupt your meal and family time, but I'm Dave Combs. I understand that the two of us will be performing at the same concert in St. Louis in September."

George graciously stood up and extended his hand warmly.

"It's great to meet you, Dave," he said before introducing me to his wife, Johnnie Lee, and one of his children. This meeting provided yet another confirmation that God had me in the right place. Another Godwink!

Linda and I caught an early morning flight to St. Louis on Saturday, September 29, 1990. When we got off the plane, we were met at the gate by a smartly dressed limo driver holding a sign that said, "Combs." Linda and I looked at each other with identical smiles. This was not an everyday thing for us—but we surely relished the moment!

Once we got settled inside the limo, we looked around with wide eyes. The stretch limo could easily seat twelve people, and it even had a bar and television!

"Linda," I said with a twinkle in my eye, "I believe this car is bigger than the first home we bought." My heart swelled with gratitude at the experiences we were given.

After checking in at the hotel, I called Jim Doyle at the radio station to let him know we had arrived—and to ask him where I might find the piano I'd be using the next day. He gave me the name and address of the local Steinway piano dealer. The limo driver took us there, where I was able to practice briefly on the *actual* Steinway concert grand piano that would be brought to the stage the next day.

Early Sunday morning, we went down to the hotel dining room for breakfast, and we noticed that The Lettermen were already there—Tony Butala, Donovan Tea, and Bobby Poynton. They greeted us and invited us to join them. We conversed warmly throughout, exchanged contact information, and promised to stay in touch.

Their limo and ours delivered us at about the same time to Buder Park, the outdoor venue for the concert, making for a surreal—and highly memorable—experience. After getting a few photos with The Lettermen, we headed to the stage to prepare for the concert.

Concert aside, the weather that day could not have been more gorgeous, with the approach of fall and a cloudless blue sky. God had put on quite a show with His creation. But now it was time for me to put on a show—with His help!

Once I saw the size of the audience, I inhaled deeply. Looking over the big park, there were people as far back as the eye could see. More than 25,000 were crowded together waiting for the performance! I told myself to exhale. *You've got this,* I said silently, knowing that the "you" I referred to was God, not me. I trusted He would speak through me as I played, as He had faithfully done before.

"'Rachel's Song' has sure come a long way from her beginnings at the church christening," I whispered to Linda. She smiled, and I could see the twinkle in her eye that confirmed she agreed.

SCHEDULE OF EVENTS

SUNDAY,
SEPTEMBER 30, 1990

BUDER PARK

9:30 a.m.	Gates Open
10:30 a.m.	Ralph Butler Band
11:45 a.m.	David Combs
1:00 p.m.	The Lettermen
2:15 p.m.	The Association
3:30 p.m.	Don McLean
5:00 p.m.	Ralph Butler Band
6:00 p.m.	George Benson

KEZK-FM102

Before I knew it, Jim Doyle from KEZK took the stage and approached the microphone to introduce me to the crowd. I was the first up to perform after a local group warmed up the audience.

KEZK announcer, Jim Doyle, came to the microphone.

"I am so excited that Dave Combs, the composer of 'Rachel's Song,' is here to perform for us today," he said in his perfect radio voice.

The crowd applauded enthusiastically.

I stepped up to the microphone and looked out at the sea of people. Parents sat with their children on lawn chairs, and couples cuddled side-by-side on blankets that seemed so close to the stage that I could have nearly touched them. The crowd stretched for what looked like a couple of football fields deep. After the first hundred feet, I couldn't make out faces; instead, the crowd almost looked like a beautiful field of colorful wildflowers moving in a gentle breeze. From where I stood, I could see ages ranging from infants to senior citizens. I thought: *Nothing brings people together quite like good food—or good music. Okay, God, let's play some good music!*

I had thought about what I'd do once I got on stage, and now it was happening—live! Breathe, I told myself as I came out to the microphone, energized by the crowd below.

"First of all, I want to thank you, Jim," I said, looking off to the side of the stage where he stood, "for inviting me to such a slice of heaven on earth." I saw the crowd appreciate this statement, their applause reinforcing my opinion of the stunning scenery.

"Second, I owe my heartfelt gratitude to *you* in the audience for voting me as a fan favorite. That touches me deeply."

The audience awarded me with applause each time I paused.

"Finally, I'm so honored to share this stage with the likes of such musical greats."

"Well, I know you're not here to listen to me talk. So, let me start my performance by playing 'Rachel's Song' for you."

I sat on the bench in front of the iconic-looking Steinway concert grand piano and let my hands briefly and gently rest on the keys. I breathed in deeply to release any nerves—and to take time to savor every moment. And then I began to play.

I heard the opening notes fill the park, and instantly I felt calm yet energized. Even as I played and the sound seemed to come from all directions—weaving itself through the crowd, around the leaves of the nearby trees, and back to me—I felt emotions similar to the first time "Rachel's Song" entered my heart and flowed through my fingers. I *lost myself* in the music, no longer consciously thinking about my fingers or the notes. The keyboard became an extension of me, and I felt a little sadness as I hit the last keys at the end of the song.

To me, this was as close to communing with God that I could come. And yet we spoke no words—just sweet, serene, angelic notes.

Even before the music faded, as if floating slowly into the open sky toward heaven, the audience exploded into applause. I rose from the piano bench to take my bows of appreciation. I could see the fans enthusiastically responding. I'd never heard such a roaring applause. That too was music to my ears.

I would not have believed it at that moment, but the day kept getting better.

After the audience enjoyed an hour of my original compositions, a representative from KEZK led Linda and me to a spacious, white autograph tent with a long table set up down and to the right of the stage where I could meet my fans, sign autographs, and sell music. As we walked towards my designated table under the tent, I noticed that The Lettermen's table was right next to mine. The Lettermen would shortly begin their performance on stage.

"It looks like we'll be sharing the tent with some great company," I told Linda as I nodded to The Lettermen's signage.

"You're right," Linda said as we got closer to my table, where I had cassette tapes and CDs stacked. "And I think we have more company joining us."

Following her eyes, I spotted what Linda had just seen. Behind the two smiling people standing at the front of my table were hundreds of people waiting behind them! I'm pretty sure my mouth dropped open. These people were standing in line to talk with me and buy my music!

"We drove all the way from Minneapolis to come hear you play," one man told me as his family stood with him at my table. "I figured this was our only chance to meet you in person. And I have to say, we would do it all over again!"

It might seem like a coincidence that my fans had come, but this was more evidence of God directing me, and me putting in the hard work to fulfill His plan. Months earlier, I had sent out a mailing to my current fan base announcing the event, but I had no idea that people would drive from as far away as Chicago, Minneapolis, and other points in the Midwest just to hear my part on the program. Nor did I ever expect they'd wait in a long line to meet me. What a humbling experience! I stood at the tent, signed autographs, gave and received hugs, posed for photographs, and talked with fans for over five hours. The only complaint at the end of the long day came from my fair skin, which didn't appreciate that I had forgotten to bring sunscreen and a hat. I ended up with a really bad sunburn—but I have to say, I'd do the whole day again, despite the pain!

Not only was the concert a once-in-a-lifetime experience for this country boy from the mountains of East Tennessee; what was even better was getting more acquainted with The Lettermen. Since our autograph tables were right beside each other, Linda and I enjoyed our ongoing discussions with the group, in between and after greeting fans.

"We always stay after every concert, as long as it takes to meet with every fan that wants to meet us," Tony Butala told Linda. Their example of appreciation and dedication to their fans made a real impression on Linda and me, and we have always tried to show our appreciation to our fans in that same caring manner.

That day launched our lifelong friendship with The Lettermen. When they came to Winston-Salem in 1995 for a concert, we hosted them for an enjoyable private lunch. In October 2019, we again enjoyed a visit with Bobby and Donovan after their concert at the Alabama Theater in Myrtle Beach, South Carolina. Tony had retired in May of 2019, and the newest member of The Lettermen, Rob Gerlach, was performing with them at the Myrtle Beach show. Linda and I enjoyed sharing some photos and fond memories of the St. Louis concert with Bobby and Donovan.

A short time after the St. Louis concert, I got one of my funniest phone calls ever from a TV station manager in the Midwest. The station had run a contest to see which of their local programs was most popular with their viewers. This was back in the time when TV stations went off the air at midnight! The regular programming would end, and the TV station would play the National Anthem and then put on the screen a test pattern of rainbow colors that they affectionately called *color bars*. Most stations would also play a single frequency tone for the sound. This particular TV station had decided to replace the tone with "Rachel's Song"! The station manager was calling me to let me know that "Color Bars" with my music had won the contest, beating out all other programming. He and I both got a real chuckle out of that news.

CHAPTER TWELVE

Concerts, New Music, and Coming Home

"When I hear your music, I am transported in spirit, heart, and soul to my safe place in the cool, dry, serene mountains."
~Mrs. Lacoure

Performing at the Columbia Baptist Church

O ur musical journey was not just reinforced by the large events—but also by our smaller, more intimate personal experiences.

While Linda and I were living in Maryland from 1988 to 1991, we were members of Columbia Baptist Church in Falls Church, Virginia. We drove the twenty-two miles to Columbia Baptist every Sunday, because we loved the music and minister so much. Columbia had wonderful choirs, organists, and pianists, plus an orchestra with several professional musicians from the National Symphony Orchestra in Washington, DC.

On our first Sunday to visit Columbia Baptist, we discovered that I had a personal connection with their minister of music, Billy Orton. As soon as I saw him, I knew he looked familiar. Turns out that he and I had both been ministers of music at the same time at different churches in Winston-Salem, North Carolina, years ago. Billy provided me the privilege of playing "Rachel's Song" on their concert grand piano as the offertory for two of their three Sunday morning services on November 11, 1990. And two weeks later, their choirs performed "In the Stillness of This Moment," a cappella (with no instrumental accompaniment), as a choral prayer. Linda had written the words, and I composed and arranged the music. I can still close my eyes and hear their beautifully blended voices softly harmonizing the notes and the prayerful words. These experiences blessed us in our own worshipful private moments and touched the congregation as well.

"In the Stillness of This Moment"
Words by Linda Combs, Music by Dave Combs

In the stillness of this moment
Fill us, fill us with Your spirit

So that we can know Your will.
In the stillness of this moment
Fill us with Your great love
So that we can show Your will.
In the stillness of this moment
Fill us, fill us with Your power
So that we can do Your will.

Celebrating Freedom—Another Defining Moment

The next summer led to another defining moment for me as well as for our country. When Iraq invaded its neighbor, Kuwait, in a brutal attack in August of 1990, President George H. W. Bush immediately began Operation Desert Shield in response. The attention of our country turned to the Middle East, and a wave of patriotism began sweeping the states.

I felt a lump in my throat and tears in my eyes that fall as we sang our national anthem at an Appalachian State University football game. Everybody in the stadium stood and sang at the top of their voices. We sounded like an enormous choir, united in the defense of freedom.

All this patriotism eventually led me to decide that my next instrumental album would be one with patriotic music. I knew there were plenty of great songs to choose from.

On Wednesday evening, January 16, 1991, I was in my hotel room in Atlanta, Georgia, on a business trip for AT&T. I had settled in for the night with the TV on. Just as the 9:00 p.m. program started, it was abruptly stopped. "We interrupt this program with a special message from the President of the United States in the Oval Office." My attention piqued.

At precisely 9:01 p.m., President George H. W. Bush addressed the nation for twelve minutes, announcing that our military had just begun the Desert Storm war to drive the Iraqi forces out of Kuwait. As he explained in great detail exactly why this action was being taken, pride and patriotism filled my being. One word repeated in my mind as I listened to President Bush tell the American people that our nation could not stand by and let Saddam Hussein take freedom away from the people of Kuwait. *Freedom! Freedom!* kept ringing in my head.

Then it hit me. I will call this album, *Celebrate Freedom*. Perfect. *That's what we all need to do—Celebrate Freedom.* After the President's message, I called Linda and told her about my inspiration.

"I think that will work really well," she immediately reinforced.

When I got home, I got busy planning the album. I picked out the songs to record, like "America the Beautiful," "God Bless the USA," "God Bless America," and of course, "The Star-Spangled Banner." Once I had my long list, I narrowed it down to thirteen. And then I got inspired and wrote one patriotic instrumental song of my own, which I called "Spirit of Peace."

In early February 1991, I sent the music to Gary Prim to allow him time to work up the arrangements. Again, Ronny Light did the engineering. In the end, the fourteen songs turned out to be beautiful and inspiring.

Back home in Maryland, I designed the original cover for the album. I wanted a patriotic message. Welcoming our soldiers home from Desert Storm with yellow ribbons was a frequent sight across the country. I bought a big yellow ribbon, tied it around an old oak tree in our backyard, crisscrossed two small American flags that we brought home from the 1990 Veterans' Day ceremony at Arlington National Cemetery, and took the cover photograph with my Nikon camera. That photo was exactly what the album needed. Of course, it was inspired by the song, "Tie A Yellow Ribbon 'Round the Old Oak Tree," written by Irwin Levine and L. Russell Brown and recorded years ago by Tony Orlando and Dawn.

I ordered 10,000 cassette tapes and 5,000 CDs of *Celebrate Freedom*. The music was shipped by Yellow Freight truck on three wooden pallets. Since I had no way to receive heavy pallets at the house, I made three trips to the trucking company in Frederick, Maryland, to bring the tapes and CDs back to our house. You should have seen my car! It was a four-door sedan, and there wasn't enough room left in the trunk, back seat, floorboards, and passenger seat to fit a mouse!

Once the new album was announced, orders immediately poured in. In the eight remaining months of 1991, I sold over 21,000 albums of *Celebrate Freedom*.

Linda and I felt it was time to give back in a bigger way a piece of what God had blessed us with. We dedicated some of the proceeds from *Celebrate Freedom* to create and endow a scholarship in the MBA program at Wake Forest University, where I had received my MBA in 1978. The Combs Celebrate Freedom Scholarship is designated for veterans of the US Armed Forces or their immediate families.

> **Linda and I felt it was time to give back in a bigger way a piece of what God had blessed us with.**

We were able to award our first scholarship in 1993, and we have since awarded scholarships to more than twenty-five recipients. These students with a military background proved to be leaders of their classes. Wake Forest School of Business had never before recruited students from the military. Today the School of Business actively recruits from military families. The value of the scholarship has more than tripled in size.

If you know of a veteran who is interested in pursuing a graduate degree in business, please encourage them to contact Wake Forest University and inquire about the Combs Celebrate Freedom Scholarship.

A Steinway to Call My Own

All the songs I wrote prior to 1991 were first played on my 100-year-old Knabe baby grand piano, which I loved to play. However, the old piano just would not hold its tune very well. I would frequently have to get out my tuning fork to tune up a few strings. This process took time away from my being creative at the piano.

"You know, Linda, we've discussed that the first major purchase we want to make for my music business is a new Steinway grand piano. I think it is time, don't you?"

Linda agreed.

So, in the spring of 1991, we decided to trade in the old Knabe and get a new Steinway. The nearest Steinway dealer was Jordan Kitt's Music in Fairfax, Virginia, about a forty-minute drive from our home in Maryland.

With great excitement and anticipation, one Saturday morning we headed for the Steinway store. As we entered the building, we were totally amazed at the enormous size of the showroom. There were seemingly hundreds of pianos.

A nicely dressed gentleman immediately greeted us with a smile and warm welcome. I explained to him that I wanted to look at Steinway B models in black finish. He ushered us over to the area where there was not just one—but *15* black, Steinway B pianos.

"Please feel free to try them out," he encouraged. That's all the encouragement I needed to sit down and play every one of them! Each piano was ever so slightly different in touch, feel, and sound. I was like a kid in a candy store.

They all sounded great, but I found one that fit me just right. It had a black satin finish with a wonderful touch and clear, beautiful sound.

"This one is it," I said. "How much is it?"

Fortunately, we had done our research, so we were not shocked at the amount. We were never big spenders, but this was my dream piano.

As part of the purchase, to help offset the expense, I traded in my old Knabe piano and the Hammond organ that I inherited from my father. *Daddy is a part of my music, yet again*, I thought as I signed the agreement.

My beautiful Steinway piano was delivered to our home in Maryland the next week. I had a few moments of sadness as they took away my Knabe piano on which I had written "Rachel's Song" and so many more. But then, the excitement set in. Like my father before me, I found that I would rather play my beautiful new piano than eat. Linda would often have to coax me off the piano for supper.

"Linda," I said after a session of playing, "I absolutely love playing our new piano." She smiled, as she always did when she saw me so happy.

Moving Back to North Carolina

In early 1991, Linda and I had some important personal and career decisions to make. Linda was the Assistant Secretary for Management for the United

States Department of the Treasury in Washington, DC, a position appointed by the President and confirmed by the United States Senate. I still worked at AT&T Network Systems in Bethesda, MD, as sales and marketing manager. And my music business with three albums was really taking off.

Linda's mother in North Carolina was having increasingly more frequent serious issues with her progressing Alzheimer's disease. Linda's father was a faithful and supportive caregiver, but the task was taking its toll on him. Linda found herself having to travel to North Carolina every couple of weeks to take care of some issue concerning her mother's health and care. Even with hired in-home assistants, it was clear that Linda's father's own health was suffering. Linda and I both felt the urgency of returning to North Carolina to be closer to family.

Before she turned in her letter of resignation, Linda had a heart-to-heart conversation with her boss, US Treasury Secretary Nicholas Brady, about her parents' health situation. He understood and supported what Linda needed to do.

I really loved my job and the wonderful people I worked with at AT&T in Maryland. My bosses at AT&T were also very understanding and supportive of our need to return to North Carolina. Linda resigned her position, and AT&T assisted me with transferring to a sales and marketing management position with North Carolina as my territory.

As if God wanted to let us know we were making the right decision, the first person who looked at our home in Maryland bought it. In April, we bought a home in Winston-Salem in the same neighborhood we moved out of in 1988.

Not only was moving a distracting and time-consuming process for us, but it also was emotionally taxing. In the three short years we'd lived in Maryland, we developed many close friendships with neighbors and colleagues. Leaving them behind was not easy. Having to depart with our wonderful office manager, Jane Wilkes, was one of the hardest parts about leaving Maryland.

Setting Up Shop in North Carolina

Jane had worked so well as office manager in Maryland, helping me free up so much time, that when we settled in North Carolina, I wasted little time looking for the right person to replace her (unfortunately, she couldn't follow us!). And by my finding the right person, I really mean *my friend Betty Wade found the right person*.

Once again, I called on my friend Betty and her Professional Office Personnel (POPI) business for help. Betty said she would send us a person as a temporary employee, and if that person didn't work out, she would find us another.

Betty sent us Betsy DeGraff, who came highly recommended and quickly exceeded our expectations. Betsy had all the qualities anyone could ask for in an office manager with her great personality, intelligence, computer savvy, and eagerness to help with the growth of Combs Music. After her eight weeks of working as a temp, we were happily able to hire Betsy full-time.

From day one, we absolutely loved having her working with us on the bottom floor of our new home. With Betsy focusing on managing the office, I could spend my time pursuing other music endeavors. And one presented itself almost immediately.

Special Performance at the Governor's Mansion

North Carolina Governor Jim Martin and his wife, Dottie, were some of the earliest people we introduced to the recording of "Rachel's Song." First Lady Dottie had immediately claimed "Rachel's Song" as her favorite song. When I received a personal invitation from Governor Martin to be one of the featured performers at the formal centennial celebration of the North Carolina Governor's Mansion in Raleigh, I was thrilled!

As a bonus, the governor invited guest performers to spend the night in the Bailey-Tucker House, the governor's guest house—a large, two-story, historic home at 213 E Lane Street across the street from the Governor's Mansion.

Linda and I arrived early that afternoon. After being greeted at the front door by one of Governor Martin's staff and entering the two-story foyer, my eyes were drawn from floor to ceiling by the impressive, spacious architecture. Looking to the left, the prominent staircase with green-carpeted steps matched the green in the floral wallpaper. White spindles supported the polished, dark-mahogany handrails. The ceilings on the first floor were so high that the long staircase led straight up—first to a landing in front of a large arched window, then turning right 180 degrees, with the remaining six steps leading to the second floor.

North Carolina Governor Jim Martin and his wife, Dottie, were some of the earliest people we introduced to the recording of "Rachel's Song."

We unpacked our luggage in our bedroom on the second floor and thought we would try and catch a short nap. We had just dozed off, when we were awakened by loud, vigorous, classical violin music just outside our bedroom door. We sat straight up in bed. It sounded like Itzhak Perlman was playing just outside our door!

Unbeknownst to us, one of the other performers had arrived before us and was staying in the bedroom across the hall. A very accomplished violinist, he must have practiced for at least a couple of hours in the house that afternoon before the performance. While we didn't get the nap we wanted, we still enjoyed his serenade.

The centennial celebration was a grand, black-tie, formal affair. As Linda and I walked across the street from the Bailey-Tucker house to the Governor's Mansion, we needed no reminder of what an honor it was to be a part of this special occasion. Governor and Mrs. Martin warmly welcomed us, as we stepped into the grand foyer. Along with a host of other dignitaries, we recognized all the living former governors in attendance: Governor (then US Senator) Terry Sanford, Governor Robert Scott, Governor James Holshouser, and Governor James Hunt.

As the program began, I got a case of the nerves. Without consciously realizing it, I rubbed my hands together and flexed my fingers to keep them warm and nimble. *Please help me to play my best, Lord*, I prayed silently.

Governor Martin introduced me when it became time for me to perform.

"I am thrilled to have my friend and the talented composer Dave Combs with us here this evening," he told the audience. "This is an especially big treat to my dear wife, Dottie, since tonight Dave will play her favorite song called 'Rachel's Song.' With that, please join me in welcoming Dave Combs."

The audience applauded as I made my way to the piano. Once the clapping died down, the room grew very still. I could almost hear my heart beating, and I wondered if the hundred-plus people in the room could see my chest thumping with each beat.

As soon as my fingers touched the keys, as had happened so many times before, I felt a wave of calm pass over me. As I played the opening notes, any remaining jitters disappeared. The sound of the music from the piano echoed beautifully throughout the spacious room. My fingers flew across the keyboard on their own wings, and once again, I almost felt like I was just along for the ride.

Once I finished "Rachel's Song," I transitioned into another couple of favorite original compositions of mine from the *Beautiful Thoughts* album. As the music flowed through my hands, I felt the familiar sensation—as if someone else played, while my emotions experienced it at my core.

Thank you, Lord, I uttered to myself.

As the last notes of the music faded, the audience responded with unrestrained applause. As I rose to take my bow of appreciation, I could see several audience members wiping tears from their eyes. They were deeply moved by the music.

This was an evening Linda and I would never forget—serving as an intimate getaway centered around our music, respected friends, and yet another once-in-a-lifetime opportunity to touch listeners through "Rachel's Song."

CHAPTER THIRTEEN

A LEAP OF FAITH

"You give so many people pleasure and will be remembered for many generations."
~RUTH

The Next Big Threshold Moment

Before long, I found myself thinking about music all the time. *Is it time for me to consider retiring from AT&T?* I hardly dared to ask myself that question.

No, I shut out that thought quickly. *No, Linda just left her career to care full time for her aging parents. We no longer have her income and benefits to fall back on. It's all on me now. You don't just walk away from a job you love, making great money and benefits.* I chided myself for even entertaining the thoughts.

I remembered the one piece of advice that my father gave me when he first learned about my job at Western Electric. He said, "David, you've got a great job with a good company. You stick with it. Don't go jumping around from job to job like I did."

But I couldn't let go of thoughts of independence—*working for myself*—something Linda and I had often talked and dreamed about.

After spending much time wrestling with my thoughts, I remembered how long I had been waiting for it to materialize. More than ten years had passed since I received and wrote "Rachel's Song." As an analytical thinker, I could spend two lifetimes thinking about pros and cons of just about any decision I might make. Fortunately, in this case, God intervened—interrupting my lonely obsession with figuring it out. Out of the blue, it dawned on me what I'd been doing wrong: Why don't you give the answer over to God? Doesn't He already know the answer?

That night, I prayed for God to show me the path I needed to take.

That night, I prayed for God to show me the path I needed to take. Then I turned it over to God, closed my eyes, and slept like a baby. My alarm clock radio woke me the next morning. Guess what song was playing on the radio? "Rachel's Song." Another Godwink.

Then came a real ah-ha moment. The following Sunday morning Linda and I were sitting quietly in the beautiful sanctuary of our church as the service began. With the spectacular rotunda ceiling overhead and the morning light streaming through the surrounding stained-glass windows, my thoughts turned to the mail I had received that week from people all over the world. These people had no idea of the decision weighing on my mind, yet somehow, they had addressed my concerns. One man wrote something that I kept thinking about over and over: "Your music is what God put you on this planet to do."

Then, I remembered recently answering the Combs Music 800 line, when the man on the phone, after placing his order with me, asked if he could say a prayer for me—which he did, right there on the phone. I was so touched. He had no idea of the decisions weighing on my mind. But God did. I still wish I had a recording of that dear man's prayer.

My thoughts turned again to how the Bible discusses using talents wisely. If you invest your talents, they'll multiply. If you don't, they'll be taken away. It's that simple.

Would I serve you better by writing and producing music? I prayed to the Lord.

During the soft music of that Sunday morning worship service, the ah-ha moment hit me. *Okay, God,* I smiled to myself. *I am listening now. Please forgive me. You must think I'm one of the densest Christians ever, Lord. You sent thousands of wonderful letters my way, and it still took me all this time to get your message. Now, I know what I need to do.*

Maybe I was expecting God to speak to me through a dramatic dream or a loud voice from the clouds. But instead, He spoke to me through other people—and He still does.

On the way home from church, I talked to Linda about what I felt I needed to do, but I expressed some concerns too.

"Does this mean I have to put out a new album or two of music each year? Because I don't know how I can do that while running the business," I told her plainly. "And what if I've already written all the songs I can write? Or what if I write more, but people don't like them?"

"Honey, you have to trust," she said in support.

The next week, I met my boss, Bill Fleenor, for lunch at Shoney's in Greensboro. This time, I wouldn't be singing in the restaurant with my high school friends—but once again, we were at that restaurant chain because of music!

On previous occasions, Bill and I had held many conversations about my music business and how the music was touching so many lives. After placing our orders, I handed Bill two inspirational letters from fans that I had received just the previous week. So, I don't think it came as any surprise to Bill when I then handed him my resignation letter.

"Bill, I'm resigning my position at AT&T to pursue my calling—writing and producing music," I told him plainly. Bill was a fine Christian man, and I witnessed the understanding in his eyes, despite any stress he may have felt in needing to shift my duties. As we talked, it was even clearer he supported my decision. Bill told me that due to corporate cutbacks, the timing of my resignation would save the job of one of my younger colleagues.

My timing—or should I say, *God's timing*—couldn't have been better. I haven't had any thoughts of regret since.

For years, I worked in information technology, ironically abbreviated as IT. Now, I would be working in lower case *it*—the *it* I had been seeking for years, involving what I was born to do. And I couldn't wait to find out where *it* might take me.

And perhaps, it didn't mean a destination point, like something you can find on a map and arrive at after hours of driving. Maybe *it* was all about the journey. In fact, I am quite certain that it was about the people and experiences that came across my path at critical times in my journey.

When I stood at this threshold, I took a bold step forward. And once I did, I accepted this moment as one that had been waiting for me the whole time.

This is what God put you on the planet to do, I thought to myself.

More Opportunities to Give Back

Once I stepped over the threshold, I had time to begin entertaining opportunities to give back.

In the spring of 1994, one such opportunity came ringing—literally, on my phone. On the other end was the soft-spoken voice of Art Unsworth, dean of the Broyhill School of Music at Appalachian State University (ASU).

"The reason for the call, Dave," he told me, "is that I've heard so much about your music business. I'm forming a new Dean's Advisory Board, and I wonder if I could interest you in coming to visit the school and learning more. I think you would make a phenomenal addition to the board as a charter member."

A few days later, Linda and I met Art over dinner. With his warm, approachable personality coupled with his love of music, he quickly won me over. He articulated a wonderful vision for the School of Music which included a music industries major for students. I eagerly accepted his invitation to serve.

That was in 1994, and I am still happily serving on that board and supporting scholarships to deserving music students.

Working Full Time to Grow Combs Music

After I left AT&T, mine and Linda's professional lives became devoted to operating and growing Combs Music, no longer distracted by other "day jobs." However, a great deal of Linda's time was spent taking care of her mother who had Alzheimer's disease and also helping her father as his health declined.

In the back of my mind, I kept thinking about my past success with the Brass Gallery at Union Station in Washington, DC. While I'd had other successes with targeting small towns with a high gift-shop-to-per-capita ratio, there was something unique about that particular shop. Sure, my persistence had paid off in spades there, since I took the time to go back again and again until they caught my vision; but I couldn't take all the credit.

I analyzed what about that shop made it so successful. The owners had a lovely location with a lot of foot traffic. Their shop was really beautiful; they sold high-quality gifts; they had constant foot traffic of new customers; and they played inviting, relaxing music.

I became determined to find more shops that had those same characteristics.

Mixing Business and Pleasure

For our twenty-fourth wedding anniversary in 1994, Linda and I treated ourselves to a weekend at the wonderful Pinehurst Hotel in Pinehurst, North Carolina. We decided to take a walk around the small quaint village of Pinehurst, like we had done in so many other tourist towns. We were always looking for good potential gift shop customers for my music.

"This village sure looks like a lot of other towns with gift shops that play and sell my music," I said to Linda.

"Hope we don't create another near riot like we did at that shop in Ellicott City," she reminisced. We both got a chuckle out of that memory. "You did bring enough music with you this time, didn't you?" she asked.

"I sure hope so."

We discovered the Potpourri gift shop at the end of one of the streets on Market Square. As soon as we walked in, I got that old, familiar feeling I had when I first entered the Brass Gallery. The store displays were eye-catching and sweet, as scented candles filled the air. While we browsed, we were greeted by a lovely woman, Eldora Wood, the owner.

"You have such a beautiful shop, Mrs. Wood," I told her sincerely. "I think this is one of the loveliest shops I've seen."

The store displays were eye-catching and sweet, as scented candles filled the air.

"Well, thank you," she beamed. "What brings you to Pinehurst?"

"We are celebrating our wedding anniversary at the Pinehurst Hotel, and we thought we'd see the village while here."

"How wonderful," she smiled. "Congratulations to the both of you. The reason I ask is that most of my customers are golf widows," she explained. "You know, when the men are out playing golf, the wives come into the shop. It's nice to see a couple come in together."

"Well, we do everything together...We even work together," I said as an opening to introduce our business.

I told her a little about our business and my music. Then I asked if she would consider playing some of my songs for her customers and selling the tapes and CDs to those who wanted the music.

"The only music I play is from that small radio," she told me, pointing to a radio on the counter.

"Your shop seems ideal for selling music," I explained. "The atmosphere is so tranquil. The longer people stay in your shop, the more likely they are to make a purchase, isn't that right?"

She agreed.

"Many shop owners tell me that my music stops people in their tracks," I continued. "Then they come to the counter to find out where to get a copy of the music playing. Once they decide on making their first purchase, they usually end up buying more things."

I could sense that this was all a new concept for her, and that she was hesitant to commit.

"Mrs. Wood," I nudged her a bit more, "I am so confident that my music will help you increase your sales, I will even purchase and install a stereo system in your shop at no cost to you."

"I don't know," she responded.

Even though she still wasn't ready to commit, I left some samples of my music with her.

"Oh, and Mrs. Wood," I said as we were leaving, "I will be back in touch soon."

As radio commentator Paul Harvey would have said, here's *the rest of the story.*

Mrs. Wood went home that evening. Over dinner with her son, Bill, she later told us that she relayed the story of meeting Linda and me at the shop. Then she told Bill about my proposition of selling tapes and

CDs in her gift shop. When she told Bill that I had also offered to put a music system in her shop for free, he incredulously said to her, "Mom! You turned him down? You have nothing to lose."

When I called Mrs. Wood the next week, she laughed, mostly at herself, when she told me what her son had said.

"So," she said, "Bill is right. I have nothing to lose. I want to take you up on your offer to install a music system and sell your music."

I headed straight to my local Radio Shack and purchased a CD player with good speakers and drove back to Pinehurst. After I installed the system, the music sounded great in her shop.

"There you go, Mrs. Wood," I said before leaving her shop. "You now have a sound system and plenty of my cassettes and CDs. I think you're going to be surprised by how your customers respond."

She *was* surprised. And so was I! I knew that my music would sell well in her beautiful shop, but I couldn't imagine just *how* well. Since that day, the Potpourri shop consistently sold more of my music than any other gift shop in the whole country, amounting to thousands of dollars.

I chose to share my music with Mrs. Wood not simply to make money, but to help transform her shop by taking it to the next level of success. My offer to install a music system in her shop seemed an easy decision to make. But it was Mrs. Wood's son, Bill, who turned this event into a confirming ah-ha moment for his mother—and for me.

CHAPTER FOURTEEN

GROWTH, *GUIDEPOSTS*, AND GOD'S GLORY

*"I just want you to know how important your music is
to me—and many other people as well."*
~MELLIE

The decade of the 1990s brought exponential growth to Combs Music, and I had the ability to release new albums and piano music books every year. However, while Combs Music came into the next level of success, life wasn't all fun and joy, especially for Linda. While I took care of most of the Combs Music business, Linda's role as caregiver for her aging parents continued to evolve. She and I talked about the seasons of life—how we had gone from being children guided by our parents to assuming a caregiving role for Linda's parents as they aged and developed health problems. Fortunately, my mama, who lived three hours away, was still quite healthy, only requiring minimal caregiving. Now it was our turn to look after the well-being of our parents.

While Linda and I spent much of our time caring for Linda's aging parents, we still experienced some incredible moments for Combs Music. During the 1990s, I released eleven music albums that included favorite hymns, favorite love songs, patriotic songs—and eighty-eight original compositions. I also published eleven piano music books to go along with the corresponding albums—seven original composition albums and four albums of favorite hymns.

Invitation from Guideposts

One of my fondest memories of the 1990s served as a defining moment I never saw coming. In the spring of 1994, I happened to be helping Betsy answer the phones one morning, when I got a call from a fan named Roberta Messner.

"I heard 'Rachel's Song' inside a gift shop, and I bought a cassette," she told me. "I cannot tell you how much that music comforted me, especially when I have bouts of pain."

As Roberta continued, she relayed to me that she suffered from a genetic disease called neurofibromatosis, once called Elephant Man's disease, an illness that requires frequent surgeries and causes excruciating pain.

"Can I ask you about how you came to write 'Rachel's Song'?" she asked.

I told Roberta the genesis of the song. When I finished, she made an unexpected request.

"What an amazing story," she said. "I am a writer for *Guideposts Magazine*, and yours is exactly the kind of inspirational story our readers love. Would you mind," she continued, "if I pitched your story to *Guideposts*?"

Do I mind!? I thought but didn't say.

"I would be honored," I told her.

Several days later, Roberta called back.

"Just as I hoped," Roberta said joyfully, "*Guideposts* is very interested in your story!"

Roberta and I scheduled several phone calls, where she conducted in-depth interviews with me. She asked questions, and I recalled as many stories as possible about my music that I could remember. A few weeks later, Roberta sent me the draft of my story for my approval, since it would be published under my byline, with Roberta acting as my ghostwriter. I approved. *I approved wholeheartedly!* In my opinion, the article was excellent, and it highlighted many things important to me like faith, family, friends, and music.

After a few weeks passed, I almost forgot about the article. Then an editor from *Guideposts* called asking if I could provide photos to accompany the article. That phone call made it all more real to me, that a magazine would actually publish my story! While I had him on the phone, I suggested that *Guideposts* might want to include information about how their readers could contact me and get my albums.

Linda took one photo of me playing the piano. Then we went out into our backyard, set up my tripod, and took a photo of Linda and me—and our grey tabby cat, Melody. Those two photos went into the mail to *Guideposts*.

Ringing Phones and Brimming Mailbags

Fast forward to late August 1994. The way we found out that the September issue of *Guideposts* hit the street was that overnight, the Combs Music phone began ringing nonstop! Caller after caller requested a copy of "Rachel's Song." With more than two million subscribers, I started wondering if all *Guideposts* readers were calling simultaneously! As soon as we hung up from one call, another took its place.

> **As soon as we hung up from one call, another took its place.**

Inundated with calls, I quickly hired two friends, Loudene Riggs and Joanie Hughes, to do nothing but sit and answer the phone all day long. Every caller wanted to place an order, and most also wanted to tell their story of how the article touched them.

When I told you that I'd share about the broader effect and stories of those touched by "Rachel's Song," this is what I meant! That small ripple that I mentioned earlier in the story was spreading into a mighty ocean.

But that wasn't all. In a couple of days, our mailman rang the doorbell. When I opened the door, he stood leaning to his right side, where he was holding the top of a large, canvas bag resting on the ground. Dragging the bag closer to me, he shook his head.

"What on earth have you all done to generate all this mail?" he asked.

He was amazed as I told him about the *Guideposts* article.

This avalanche of mail lasted for days. We got so much mail one day that we couldn't even begin to read the letters. Linda and I stayed up all night just zipping open the envelopes. Talk about a nice problem to have. Almost every envelope had a note or letter—and a check for $10 for a copy of the cassette.

During a couple of weeks, we heard from more than 10,000 people—surpassing our wildest imagination for the interest that the article, and my music, could generate. This kept me making several trips each day to the post office with my car full (trunk, back seat, and front passenger seat!) of mail bins with filled orders. While the number of calls and letters eventually slowed down, they didn't really go away. Even years later, someone would find that issue of *Guideposts* in a doctor's office waiting room, and I would get another letter.

Funny, even though we no longer live at that address, and the change of address has long run out, the postman still remembers Combs Music. Because we still live on that same route, he still delivers our mis-addressed mail to our current address.

I am eternally grateful to the dear-hearted Roberta Messner, whose instincts led her to take the initiative to share the story of "Rachel's Song" with millions of readers. This story launched Combs Music on an even higher trajectory, which would last for years to come.

The Day the Phones Stopped Ringing

Sales of music remained robust following the 1994 *Guideposts* article. That led Combs Music to a record Christmas season, and our future never looked brighter—until January 24, 1995. To me, January 24 will always be remembered as "the day the phones stopped ringing."

Do you remember what was going on in our nation—and the world—on January 24, 1995? On that day, America got introduced to the first live reality television of its kind, the live coverage of the O.J. Simpson murder trial. And subsequently, the 1990s brought about the mesmerizing effect of real-time, live drama on TV.

And the effect on Combs Music was unmistakable. Where we normally fielded dozens of calls each day from customers and gift shops placing orders, our phones remained eerily quiet. As America stayed held in the grip of real-life drama, many potential customers were obviously riveted to their televisions.

This live media coverage killed music phone sales for nine months, and music sales in general never fully recovered. Since the advent of 24-7 news coverage, Americans were deluged with distractions and the TV viewing habits of some viewers were permanently changed. As a culture, many Americans seemed to be moving away from the relaxing sounds of soothing, pensive music.

But Fortunately, the Music Didn't Stop Everywhere

Throughout 1995, I stayed busy performing "Rachel's Song" at church services and civic clubs. In early February, I got a phone call from our longtime friend, Loudene Riggs.

"You know, Dave," she said, "I can't stop thinking about all the touching stories I heard from your fans when I helped answer phone calls from the Guideposts article."

"That is so sweet to hear, Loudene," I told her. "Thank you sincerely for your help. You helped us through a really busy time."

"And that got me thinking," she said as I could hear her taking in a breath. "Would you consider offering a Sunday evening concert at our church?"

Loudene's husband, Paul, was the pastor of Oaklawn Baptist Church in Kernersville, North Carolina. The church had recently built a beautiful, modern sanctuary which could seat nearly 900 people. I could picture the layout of the church, and I could almost hear the acoustics carrying my music into so many ears.

My immediate thoughts made me doubt whether I could do something of this magnitude. I remembered how nervous I had been five years ago performing in St. Louis for 25,000 people. However, Loudene's excitement and vision for this concert was contagious.

"Okay," I said before we hung up. "I'll do it under one condition. You have to help me."

I knew a full-length program would require a host of musicians—pianist, organist, and singers. I shared with Loudene my thoughts on what I would need.

"How about the musicians at First Baptist Church in Mocksville, North Carolina?" she said almost immediately. "Paul served as minister there for nearly ten years."

I remembered performing "Rachel's Song" as an offertory for a Sunday morning worship service at that church, so I was familiar with the quality of their musicians. Their organist, Donna Lanier, had accompanied me. Loudene reminded me that their minister of music, Lewis Phillips, was also very accomplished on organ and piano. Donna was also an excellent pianist.

"Okay, Loudene," I laughed. "It seems you've thought of everything. I'll start working on my end, if you can get Lewis and Donna to join the team."

In no time, Loudene's passion had persuaded Donna and Lewis to perform for the concert.

We set the concert date for Sunday evening, March 19, at 7:00 p.m. Next came the selection of the music for the concert. At this point, I had already published the piano music books for the *Rachel's Song* and *Beautiful Thoughts* albums. And the piano music for several of the songs on the *September Psalm* album had been transcribed. Collectively with Donna and Lewis, we chose my songs from a wide selection and laid out the order for the concert.

I wanted the program to be more than just a concert. It would be a Sunday evening worship service, complete with an offertory hymn—and a collection for the church (not for me).

Next, I started getting the word out about the concert. Many of my fans had told me that if I ever did a public performance to please let them know. Using a software application called GeoQuery, I sorted through the more than 23,000 names from my database of fans who had ordered music from me, selecting those living within a 200-mile radius. I designed an invitation postcard and mailed it to nearly 3,000 people. Knowing the church would hold only about 900 people, I was hoping that I could at least fill up the sanctuary.

On the evening of the concert, Linda and I arrived at the church around 6:00 p.m., and Loudene, Paul, and the musicians arrived shortly thereafter. For the concert, the church had printed 1,000 copies of the program for the ushers to hand out as people entered. Inside the sanctuary, the pulpit had been replaced by the grand piano in the center of the platform. The musicians and I warmed up a little and tested out the microphones. Everything sounded great. The piano resonated with rich tones, blending nicely with the organ.

Although the concert started at 7:00 p.m., people arrived shortly after 6:00 p.m., and by 6:45 p.m. the sanctuary was full!

Music from my *Springtime Reflections* CD had been playing over the sound system, as the prelude music to set the tone for the concert. Feeling the anticipation from the audience, my nerves hit me.

As I sat with Linda in the front pew, I moved my fingers quickly to keep them limber and fast. It also gave me something to do with my jitters!

Promptly at 7:00 p.m., Loudene stepped up to the microphone.

"I want to thank you all for coming tonight," she said warmly. "We are so privileged to have Donna Lanier and Lewis Phillips from Mocksville Baptist Church playing piano and organ throughout the concert. And of course, I want to introduce you to the man and his music, the reason why you are here this evening."

The more personal, kind things Loudene said about me, the more nervous I became! In fact, I got so nervous and excited to play "Rachel's Song," I rose from my seat and went to the piano as the audience applauded, completely forgetting that a quartet from Mocksville Baptist planned to sing a call to worship that I had written called "In the Stillness of This Moment." As soon as I saw the quartet standing in front of their microphones, I reached for my microphone and apologized to the audience.

"Sorry," I smiled. "I got a little ahead of myself! Before I play, let's enjoy the call to worship by the Mocksville Baptist Church quartet."

And I have to say, we all did enjoy their ethereal singing in a cappella (with no instrumental accompaniment), as their voices blended to create the sounds of heaven.

When it was time for me to play "Rachel's Song," I caught Linda's eye as she gave me her smile of confidence and love. As my hands approached the keys, I silently asked God to help me play my best, and I felt the nerves lose their grip on me.

As my hands approached the keys, I silently asked God to help me play my best, and I felt the nerves lose their grip on me.

While my hands moved effortlessly around the keys, I heard the complementing sounds of the organ skillfully played by Donna Lanier. The two instruments sounded almost as one as the music rose above the stage, reached the height of the arched ceiling, and in gentle waves, washed over the audience.

Since virtually all the audience had heard a recording of "Rachel's Song" before, I could sense their anticipation as the music rose to a crescendo modulation at the end of verse two and launched into verse three, up a half step to the key of D flat. As I struck the final keys at the end of "Rachel's Song," I let the notes of the piano sustain until they faded completely away—before releasing the sustain pedal. Then I rose from the bench and turned to the audience as they applauded in appreciation.

At that moment, I knew the rest of the program would be remarkable.

Donna on the piano and Lewis on the organ performed three songs from my *Beautiful Thoughts* album, before I returned to the piano and played the title song, "Beautiful Thoughts."

For the offertory hymn, I had chosen "O for a Thousand Tongues to Sing." God must have inspired that choice, because little did I know when I chose this hymn that there would be nearly a thousand voices singing at the concert. Hearing the hymn was indeed a heavenly experience.

After the offertory, Charles Walker from Mocksville Baptist sang a solo of "King of Kings is Born"—the song written by my father, Joe Combs, which had an instrumental version on my *First Christmas* album. My heart soared as I imagined how proud Daddy would have been to hear his song performed so beautifully.

Donna and Lewis then played duets of three songs from my *September Psalm* album. I concluded the program by performing "Reflections on Still Water" from my *Beautiful Thoughts* album. After a prayer of benediction, the congregation sang "God's Great Family," a short chorus which I had written and was printed on the back of the program. The congregation had so many strong, beautiful voices that their 1,000 voices sounded more like 10,000.

This was the most memorable worship service I had ever attended. Every voice and instrument rang out the glory of God, and I could feel a spirit of joy fill the room as we sang the final song. I felt transported to a heavenly place, and judging by the energy in the audience, I think others did too. The music seemed to transcend earthly reality, bathing us with God's blessings and joy.

After the concert, we walked to the fellowship hall, where I had an opportunity to greet everyone. We enjoyed refreshments, and I met members of the audience at the table where I sold cassettes, CDs, and piano music books. I signed so many autographs that night that my hand was sore for a week!

One family came from Virginia. Others told me they traveled for hours on church buses to attend.

"Thank you so much for sending us the postcard invitation," one fan told me. "We drove here from South Carolina to meet you and hear your music."

I took my time with each person who stopped by to talk with me. One by one, they told me how *touched they were by the music*—and how much they enjoyed the concert.

Before I went to sleep that night, I thanked God for how he continued to tune me and put me where He could be glorified.

CHAPTER FIFTEEN

THE POWER OF POSITIVE PARTNERSHIPS

"Had you had dinner at our house last evening, you would have heard pianist Gary Prim playing original music by Dave Combs—soft, subtle, beautiful original music so that there are no familiar lyrics to intrude on your revelry or on our conversations.... Start with the one called 'Quiet Escapes,' and eating becomes dining."
~PAUL HARVEY,
AMERICAN RADIO BROADCASTER AND NATIONAL TREASURE

Letters from Paul Harvey and Others

Every note or letter I have received is special. Going to my mailbox (and in recent years, my email and voice mail boxes) every day remains a joyful experience. I've gotten notes from young people, senior citizens, piano players, ministers, doctors, nurses, teachers, and people describing themselves as "just ordinary folks" who were touched by this music. I cherished the personal notes I got in the mail from the now-late Paul Harvey telling me that he and his wife, Angel, enjoyed playing my music for dinner each evening. Then, much to my surprise, Paul Harvey mentioned my music on his radio program a couple of times, and our 800 number went wild once again!

Then, much to my surprise, Paul Harvey mentioned my music on his radio program a couple of times, and our 800 number went wild once again!

When gift shop owners started carrying my music, many expressed their surprise to me over the positive, emotional reactions from those who'd heard the music in their stores. I never stopped feeling honored and blessed by those comments, but I was never surprised. I'd also seen and heard firsthand how the music touched people—from notes like the grieving parent listening by car radio and needing to be comforted, to the inspirational words from fans at large music venues.

Even today, when customers call the Combs Music 800 number to place an order, most of them want to share a story telling how they found the music and how it made them feel. I cherish each story. You can read more of these stories in Chapter 21.

The Temple of God Cantata

Sometimes God uses the storms in our lives to help us get quiet with Him—so he can whisper to us about our next steps. Those storms may be difficult times—or literally, winter hazards.

The blizzard of 1996 hit the East Coast the first week of January. In Winston-Salem, we don't usually get much snow, but we often get freezing rain and ice. That storm accumulated such thick, heavy ice on our trees that the sound of large limbs snapping off and hitting the ground sounded like gunfire just outside our windows. We kept our eyes on the large trees all around our home from the picture windows on two sides of our house, and we prayed no falling limbs would come crashing through a window.

Then our power went off.

"I guess we can light some candles," I told Linda.

And that worked well for the rest of the day. Unfortunately, we ran out of candles by the time the power returned twelve days later! Thankfully, our gas fireplace kept us from freezing, as we ran it around the clock. Even with our fireplace, the house became frigid. How cold was it, you ask? It was so cold that Melody, our cat, who never had been a lap cat, jumped into my lap and snuggled up to me as I sat next to our fireplace.

To preserve our food, we emptied the contents of our freezer into a cooler and put it outside in the frigid temperatures to keep it from spoiling. Ever-resourceful Linda made some of the best chicken and dumplings I have ever had by cooking them the old-fashioned way in a pot over the flames in the fireplace.

The meal wasn't the only wonderful creation that came out of that frigid weather. That same year, our church, First Baptist Church in Winston-Salem, would celebrate its 125th anniversary. Our minister of music, Jim

Bailiff, had approached me a few weeks earlier about the possibility of me writing some special music to celebrate the anniversary. As Linda and I sat near the fireplace to stay warm, I had time to consider his request.

"I've been thinking about the church's anniversary, but I haven't gotten any real inspiration for words or music."

"Well, how about this?" she offered as a question. "I'd be happy to write some words based upon the Scriptures about the Temple of God in the Old Testament."

I didn't need to think long.

"If you write the words, I'll write the music," I told her with renewed inspiration.

Linda wrote two or three songs so quickly that she came up with another idea.

"Why don't we just write an entire cantata?"

That's my bride—beautiful, resourceful, creative, and driven!

Over the next two weeks, Linda wrote ten songs. We didn't need electricity to make our musical collaboration work. Linda just needed a pen and paper, and I could write at the piano even without power. We took advantage of those twelve days without power to write what we decided to name *The Temple of God* cantata. The time dedicated solely to creating music with my wife felt like a sacred gift—in the shelter of our home, amidst the coldest of days.

> **The time dedicated solely to creating music with my wife felt like a sacred gift—in the shelter of our home, amidst the coldest of days.**

I wrote the music during those chilly, powerless days. But when power finally returned, I used my Kurzweil synthesizer to develop the orchestral accompaniments for the ten songs. Then I worked to incorporate all the components of our church music programs into the cantata—adult choir, youth choir, soloist, praise quartet, children's choir, handbell choir, organ, piano, and Kurzweil synthesizer. After hours on my computer and synthesizer, I engraved the entire music to make it ready for printing, later presenting the cantata to Jim Bailiff.

He loved it.

We spent weeks lining up the musicians and rehearsing the cantata. Some of the most challenging yet memorable rehearsals were with the children's choir. I had spent years working with adults, not little people with attention spans measured in seconds. This experience raised my appreciation of those who work with children full-time! Even though the children's choir made progress, I must admit I was a little worried about their part of the cantata.

On the Friday before the Sunday performance, we held our first full rehearsal with over 100 performers. I worked with the children's choir first, so that their parents could get them home early.

I watched as the children lined up on the platform in front of the adult choir. Several fidgeted about or leaned so heavily on one foot that I feared they would topple over. A few poked their neighbors. In other words, they were just being kids!

Finally, I began their song, "In God's Garden." The organ, piano, and synthesizer played a ten-bar instrumental introduction, and then the adult choir started singing the first verse. I looked over at the children. I will never forget the looks on their faces as they stood just a few feet in front of the adult choir. Their mouths opened in awe, their eyes widened, and they turned their heads to see where this heavenly music was coming from. I could just read their minds: *Wow! So, this is what music is supposed to sound like.* From that moment on, they gave me their undivided attention.

Since the cantata commemorated the celebration of the church's founding, I wanted as many of the church members to participate as possible. I invited anyone who had ever sung in the choir to join us for this performance. Many did.

Every time I watch the video of the performance, I am touched by how many of those special people are no longer with us. People like Earline Heath King—wonderful singer and entertainer in her younger years, famous sculptor in her later years, and dear friend with whom I shared the same birthday.

The premier performance of *The Temple of God* was at 3:00 p.m. on Sunday, September 15, 1996. Nearly 1,000 people attended—church members, friends, and family, including Linda's eighty-two-year-old father, Robert Morrison. First Baptist Church—with its beautiful rotunda style sanctuary—was full, even the balcony. It was very exciting to see the sanctuary filled to capacity. All the musicians performed beautifully, and the audience was deeply moved. Linda and I felt honored to contribute to such a celebration.

The Joy of Blowing Rock, North Carolina

Once I had opened accounts with gift shops to sell my music, I didn't consider my work to be done. I loved the relationships I developed with store owners and managers, and I did everything I could to support them. Sometimes, that meant traveling to their towns to get personally involved and meet their customers.

Blowing Rock, North Carolina, became one of our favorite small tourist towns to visit. It consisted mostly of just one main street, about four blocks long, lined with quaint little gift shops. Early on, as I've shared, I realized that this was the ideal kind of town to play and sell my music. At about 3,500 feet elevation, it was cool and pleasant in the summer, attracting thousands of visitors, especially on weekends. The sidewalks on both sides of the street were usually filled with tourists leisurely strolling, window-shopping, and going into shops when something caught their eye. Every day in Blowing Rock brought an abundance of new out-of-town visitors.

One of my favorite shops there was The Basket Boutique. The owners, Alan and Laura Packer, were loyal customers (and wonderful people), and I wanted to do anything I could to boost their sales. I always accepted their invitations to spend a day meeting their customers and autographing music purchases. Their shop had a welcoming, full front porch complete with rocking chairs, a swing, and white Chippendale railing. I would set up my music display table on the porch and play my CDs on my Bose Music System—just loud enough to be heard ten feet away on the sidewalk.

Typically, I would see a family leisurely walking down the sidewalk, and as they approached the front walkway, they would stop, look up to the porch where the music played, and climb the steps. Nearly every one of them would purchase music.

Laura told me, "Whenever I play 'Rachel's Song,' customers rave about it. Clearly, it touches almost everyone." At the end of the day, I could sense the owners' gratitude at the spike in sales.

Doing personal appearances was one of my favorite ways to promote my music. Usually, the shop also got a publicity article in the local newspaper, *The Blowing Rocket*, prior to my appearance. But more than the sales or publicity, these seemingly small experiences filled our lives with joy—reminding us that we were living God's plan.

Blue Ridge Parkway Video Made for PBS

His plan found new uses—and new media—for my music. In early 2000, I got a phone call from Rob Van Camp, who wanted to know if I would be willing to license him for the use of some of my music for a special video that he was filming as a fundraiser for North Carolina Public Television, UNC-TV.

"I'm filming a 45-minute program about the Blue Ridge Parkway," he told me, "And I can't think of any music more fitting and beautiful than yours."

Rob told me that David Holt, a well-known North Carolina musician and storyteller, would narrate the film. I knew that any video that Rob produced would be Emmy Award-winning quality. He and David were North Carolina treasures.

I didn't have to think long about his request.

"Linda and I have always loved driving along the Blue Ridge Parkway. I would be honored to have my music played throughout your video production."

Rob selected music from my *Rachel's Song* and *Springtime Reflections* albums—songs like "Abundant Joy," "Crystal Clear Stream," "May Flowers," and "Bluebirds Singing." His videography of the Parkway was stunning—with long-range views looking down on the valleys below and aerial shots showing the Parkway snaking its way along the mountainsides. Watching the video just made me want to jump in the car and take another leisurely ride on the Parkway. I couldn't have been more pleased with the final product. The video program helped increase the visibility of The Blue Ridge Parkway as a national treasure and one of the most visited national parks. It also helped to raise many thousands of dollars to support UNC-TV.

CHAPTER SIXTEEN

A Blessed Union

"God has truly used your talents in composing to make the most beautiful music we have ever listened to. We used '
Rachel's Song' in our wedding repertoire and played it continually while on our honeymoon. It has a very special place in our hearts."
~ANTOINETTE

New Friends—Actually Best Friends Forever (BFFs)

The connections and partnerships launched by "Rachel's Song" continued....

Linda and I first met Bob and Jane Handly back in the early 1990s through a phone call to our home.

"Is this the Linda Combs who wrote the book, *A Long Goodbye*?" the sweet Southern voice asked Linda.

"Yes, it is."

"And is your husband the one who wrote, 'Rachel's Song?'" the caller asked a second question.

"Yes."

"This is Jane Handly. We've never met, but I know all about you. My mother is Rachel Carter, and she talks about you all the time."

Linda told Jane how much she loved and admired her mother, Rachel.

Rachel Carter was the highly respected and loved former head of reading education for the Winston-Salem Forsyth County School System and worked closely with Linda when she was a reading coordinator in the 1970s. Linda knew about Jane from her many conversations with Rachel, but Linda and Jane had never physically met.

After the two of them caught up, Jane explained the reason for the call. On a recent visit to North Carolina to visit her parents, Jane had purchased one of Linda's books, *A Long Goodbye*, which Linda had written about her journey of caregiving for her mother who had

Alzheimer's disease. Jane said that in the bookstore, she sat down on the floor to begin reading it, and she couldn't stop the tears from flowing. Jane's dear mother, Rachel, had the beginning signs of dementia.

On that same trip home, Jane had taken her mother to shop in Old Salem. As Jane and Rachel browsed through the Moravian Gift and Book Shop with all its wonderful sights and smells, beautiful instrumental music began playing in the shop. At the checkout counter, Jane found out that the music was "Rachel's Song."

"This song was written specifically for me," Rachel told Jane, who compassionately did not even attempt to question her statement. Jane bought one copy for herself and one for Rachel.

Back home in Dallas, Jane started playing her CD of "Rachel's Song" on their stereo. Her husband, Bob, was upstairs. When he heard the music, he immediately came downstairs.

"What is that music you are playing?" he asked.

"It's called 'Rachel's Song.' I bought it while visiting my mother."

They were both brought to tears as the song filled their home. Then Jane showed Bob the book, *A Long Goodbye.* They noticed that the last names on the book and CD were Combs. And the address on the CD and the book was *Winston-Salem.*

> **They were both brought to tears as the song filled their home.**

"We have to talk to these people," they agreed. Bob looked up our phone number, and they placed the call. Bob and Jane quickly became two of our dearest friends in the whole world—who we still love "to the moon and back," as Jane is fond of saying. We appreciate their outward success. Bob and Jane are both award-winning public speakers. Bob is the author of four best-selling books and plays a great game of golf. Jane, "beautiful on the inside and outside" as her mother used to say, is a former Miss Winston-Salem. But more than that, we appreciate their heart for God—and their everlasting friendship.

God's orchestra sometimes expands through grand gestures, drawing thousands of people overnight; other times, it grows in subtle, almost silent ways—with members who last a lifetime.

Co-Writing of "You Were Worth the Wait"

God wasn't done adding to the orchestra that would join my life. No matter where we went, it seemed that music—like God—went before us, and followed us....

Fast-forward to January of 2000. Linda and I learned that Miles Warfford, Jane Handly's son, had gone to Greece with his girlfriend, Pauletta. At the stroke of midnight—New Year's Eve 1999—Miles asked Pauletta to marry him. While many people feared that civilization would end at midnight as the calendar rolled from 1999 to 2000 (Y2K), Miles decided instead to bet on the future.

"If civilization is going to end, we might as well be where it all began," Miles explained his reasoning behind getting engaged in Greece. They set their wedding date for September 2000 and began making plans.

Linda and I were invited to attend another wedding in Bob's and Jane's family in late April 2000 for Jane's niece—Miles's first cousin. That weekend in Winston-Salem never looked more beautiful—with azaleas, rhododendron, and peonies in full bloom, showing off their best spring colors.

Bob and Jane had flown in from Texas and were picking up their close friend, Jana Stanfield, at the airport. Jana is a multitalented singer/songwriter/speaker who Linda and I had met at previous National Speakers Association events. Jana was to sing a couple of special songs, including one that she wrote, at the wedding that weekend.

Bob loved to plan ahead, with great attention to detail. On the way from the airport to Winston-Salem, Bob was driving—with Jane in the front passenger seat, and Jana in the back seat. Bob was already thinking—not about that weekend's wedding, but of the September wedding.

"How about writing a special song for Miles and Pauletta that you could sing at their wedding?" Bob asked Jana, seemingly out of the blue.

"Bob, you can't just order up a song," Jana laughed. "It doesn't work that way. Let me think about it."

After the wedding ceremony where Jana sang her two lovely songs, she approached me at the reception with an idea.

Jana said, "I've been thinking about Bob's request for a song for Miles and Pauletta. I have jotted down some tentative words. I've heard Jane many times describe how she had prayed for years that the right young woman would come along and settle down her somewhat free-spirited son. Jane just knew that Pauletta was the answer to her prayers."

Those thoughts had inspired the words Jana had written down on a small piece of paper entitled, "You Were Worth the Wait."

When the reception progressed into what I call the "loud music and dancing" phase, I suggested that Linda, Jana, and I exit the party and go to our house to work on the song. At about 9:30 p.m., I sat on the piano bench at my Steinway grand piano, and Jana joined me on my right.

"Your words are so lyrical and touching," I told Jana. "They make me feel something like this...." I immediately started playing a minor key chord, and a melody that flowed with the words. The two of us got goosebumps! Then Jana sang the melody, her sweet voice inspiring the next phrase of the song even before I played it.

I had only once before witnessed a song come together so naturally. In forty-five minutes, we had the whole song done. That's how inspiration works.

"You Were Worth the Wait"

There were times when I almost gave up,
Believing that things could change,
Times when I nearly lost faith,
But just look at us here today.

Chorus:
You were worth the wait,
Worth every twist of fate,
Worth every prayer I prayed,
You were worth the wait,
You were worth the wait.

I was searching for you for so long,
Desperately lonely for miles,

But all of the heartache and pain,
Is forgotten when I see you smile.

Bridge:
Think of the joy we might've missed,
The laughter of children,
A lifetime together,
A moment like this.

Writing it was easy. But would we be ready to play it at the wedding, just months away?

Preparing for a Blessed Wedding

This song we wrote was intended as a surprise gift for Miles and Pauletta from Bob and Jane. Writing it was certainly a pleasant surprise for Jana and me, since it practically fell together, as if we were transcribing a song we'd both known forever. I mean the song practically wrote itself!

But to get it ready for the wedding, it needed to be professionally recorded in the studio. Fortunately, I had friends in musical places!

I called Gary Prim, who was delighted to work on the arrangement and accompaniment. Then I sent him the lead sheet for the music. Next, I booked studio time in Studio A at Reflections studios in Berry Hill, the same studio I had used many times before. Then I called my expert recording engineer, Ronny Light. The day before the session, Linda and I drove to Nashville while Bob and Jane flew in from Dallas. Jana Stanfield had a short commute since she lived in Nashville at the time. Is this all sounding a bit familiar? It felt good to be "back in the saddle" with my recording friends and colleagues.

We all rendezvoused at the studio. Gary's synthesizer rack and keyboard had already been delivered and set up by the cartage company that he used. After making all the introductions, we were ready to make some music!

Ronny had all the studio equipment hooked up and ready to record. Gary and Jana sat in the main studio at the piano, determining in which key Jana was most comfortable singing the song. A highly skilled musician, Gary used the Nashville numbering system to notate his music, so he could easily play any song in any key.

Bob, Jane, Linda, and I watched from the control room—soaking up all this activity. I reflected on my first time in the studio, recording "Rachel's Song." I felt incredibly blessed, as I looked around the studio on this day years later—surrounded by friends and colleagues who had become friends.

Since this was Bob's and Jane's first time in a recording studio, they could hardly contain themselves—and the recording hadn't even yet begun! Even though Linda and I were never blessed with children, I imagine the anticipation of waiting for the birth of a child was a bit like how we felt waiting to birth this new song.

After some preliminary testing of microphone levels, Gary, Jana and Ronny were ready to begin the recording in earnest. Sometimes, it takes a bit of practice for musicians to build their confidence in the recording studio. Not so with these professionals. Gary and Jana were ready to unleash their talents at full strength. Ronny recorded it all, and after a few takes, everyone felt pleased with the results. Jana returned to the studio to record some two-part harmony on a separate track. When she finished, Gary took his place and recorded more accompaniment tracks of the other instruments using his synthesizer, adding lush sounding strings and an oboe.

> Sometimes, it takes a bit of practice for musicians to build their confidence in the recording studio. Not so with these professionals.

We all sat in the control room as Ronny worked his magic, mixing Jana's voice along with Gary's piano and the other accompaniment instruments in perfect balance. We all sat mesmerized.

That's it, I thought, as the music came together.

When Ronny played it back for us, we all had tears flowing down our faces. We were blown away, overwhelmed at how beautiful and touching the music sounded when all the elements came together. None of us at Studio A that day will ever forget those moments.

Bob and Jane intended this song as a surprise for Miles and Pauletta. Well, that was the plan. But Bob and Jane couldn't wait until the wedding! Weeks later, when Miles and Pauletta flew to Dallas to visit Bob and Jane, Bob and Jane played the recording of "You Were Worth the Wait" for the young couple. From the first chords, Miles and Pauletta were overwhelmed, speechless, and in tears. Bob and Jane overflowed with joy, knowing they had given their "kids" the gift of a lifetime.

On Miles's and Pauletta's wedding day, I played a selection of my original music on the piano for the prelude. As the mothers were seated, I played "Rachel's Song" on the piano. After the exchange of vows and rings and the wedding prayer, Jana sang "You Were Worth the Wait" from the balcony to Gary Prim's accompaniment. As her beautiful voice filled the large sanctuary, there was not a dry eye in the house. Then the wedding concluded with the marriage pronouncement by the minister, Dr. Ritchel.

If you'd like to share in what that sounded like on the wedding day, you can find a music video of "You Were Worth the Wait" on YouTube. Type "You Were Worth the Wait combsmusic" into the search field. The entire song will play with some of my photography in the background, while the lyrics display on the screen. Or just scan this QR code.

CHAPTER SEVENTEEN

More Orchestras, Programs, A Shifting Nation, and Moving Pictures

"I am a psychotherapist, [I have found that] 'Rachel's Song' helps me stay present and in touch and...creates a safe and nurturing space for whatever needs to happen for clients."
~ELIZABETH

More Orchestras Perform "Rachel's Song"

The music kept growing with a life of its own. In October of 2000, the Anderson South Carolina Symphony Orchestra performed "Rachel's Song" as a piano concerto featuring Dr. James Clark as pianist. Unfortunately, Linda and I were unable to attend this pops concert by this community orchestra. I received a letter from a fan who attended the concert. She said that "Rachel's Song" was wonderful, bringing tears as she closed her eyes and soaked in the beauty of the music.

You never know where a seemingly chance encounter will lead.

You never know where a seemingly chance encounter will lead.

On a beautiful, fall Saturday Linda and I were in Blowing Rock, North Carolina, for the Art in the Park weekend along with thousands of tourists in town for this monthly event. We were there for the day as guests of the owners of the Basket Boutique located on Sunset Drive. As usual, they set up a table for me on the front porch with my tapes, CDs, and portable Bose Music System—playing my music just loud enough to be heard on the sidewalk. All day long, tourists stopped by to listen to and purchase my music.

At one point, I looked up the street and recognized our good friends, Frank and Kay Borkowski, strolling down the sidewalk while chatting with another couple. Frank served as the Chancellor of Appalachian State University, and Kay and I sat together on the board of advisors for the Dean of the School of Music at ASU.

Frank and Kay looked up and spotted Linda and me about the same time that we saw them. Bounding up the steps to the porch, they greeted us and introduced us to their friends, Dr. Einar Anderson and his wife, Susan, from Columbia, South Carolina. This would turn into another Godwink moment.

"Einar has two jobs, really," Frank explained. "He's both a surgeon as well as the music director for the South Carolina Philharmonic Orchestra."

"You know," Kay turned to Einar, "you might be interested to know that Dave has a symphony arrangement of 'Rachel's Song' that's already been performed locally. I wonder if that's something that your orchestra could perform as well."

"I am always interested in presenting beautiful music," he said genuinely.

The two of us exchanged contact information before the four of them continued with their day.

Dr. Einar Anderson was sincere, indeed. In the Spring of 2001, Linda and I drove to Columbia, South Carolina, to attend his performance of "Rachel's Song" by the South Carolina Philharmonic Orchestra on the campus of the University of South Carolina. Sitting near the front, Linda and I watched as Dr. Anderson conducted the flawless performance of "Rachel's Song." The music washed over my soul like it had the first time the simple melody played inside my head. As always, the music touched everyone in attendance, and I was ever grateful for God's grace in letting me share my music.

Program for Winston-Salem Rotary

Sometimes we followed God's call to audiences in sweeping auditoriums, and other times, we led programs in smaller venues to spread "Rachel's Song." One of those times was in June of 2001. Linda is a Rotary life member, and she and I presented a joint program for her local Rotary Club. I played "Rachel's Song" and several of my other original songs on the piano. In between songs she told my stories. As usual, these appearances were lots of fun. I loved tag teaming with Linda.

Post 9/11 Feedback from
Use of Celebrate Freedom *Music*

Any American who lived through 9/11 could tell you where they were when the planes hit the Twin Towers—and later the Pentagon. Having previously lived in the Washington, DC area, it felt particularly real to us—as we watched with our whole nation.

This can't be happening here, I thought as I stood in disbelief, riveted to the news on the television in the Combs Music area of our home in Winston-Salem.

Linda was watching from a different view. Even though we were living in North Carolina, Linda was still connected to many government leaders in our nation's capital. She was in her car on her way to an important meeting with some of these leaders in Washington, DC, very close to the Pentagon that morning. She actually saw the smoke rising from the Pentagon and the fighter jets screaming overhead at very low altitude. I immediately tried but was unable to reach her by cell phone, as I was really worried about her. She eventually called home on a landline from a car dealership, letting me know she was okay and was heading back home. This tragedy touched our family up close and personal.

The days and weeks following the tragic terrorist attack brought raw emotions, as we all experienced the early stages of grief—denial and anger. *Our freedom had come under attack.* Young students particularly struggled to comprehend and process what had just happened.

On the Saturday following 9/11, I received an email from a Wisconsin schoolteacher about what my *Celebrate Freedom* music meant to her family and their local middle school students and teachers. The year before, she had given this CD to the principal of the middle school to use in a national Blue Ribbon school celebration. After 9/11, recognizing the students' and faculty's need for something

> **The days and weeks following the tragic terrorist attack brought raw emotions, as we all experienced the early stages of grief—denial and anger.**

uplifting to support our nation, the principal began playing the CD on the school PA system before every announcement.

The teacher said the music had a *profound, soothing effect* on both students and staff. They had a large remembrance assembly, where students and staff read thoughts they had prepared in response to 9/11. The music from Celebrate Freedom also was played in the background while people read. She reported there wasn't a dry eye in the gym.

Guest Conductor for the
Gardner-Webb University Symphony

In 2001, Stephen Plate, the chair of the Department of Fine Arts at Gardner-Webb University (GWU), invited me to be the guest conductor for the performance of "Rachel's Song" by the GWU Symphony Orchestra at their Christmas concert.

I'd be honored, I thought, as I considered what a special place GWU was to Linda—having attended her first two years of college there—and later to both of us. In 1985, Linda received the alumnus of the year award. And in 1987, Linda gave the commencement address and was awarded an honorary Doctor in Humanities degree. Later, in 2000 and 2001, Linda and I both served briefly on the Board of Trustees of GWU.

The Christmas concert at GWU began with John Phillip Sousa's rousing arrangement of "The Star-Spangled Banner." Tears welled in my eyes, hearing the entire audience singing our national anthem with such enthusiasm and patriotism. *It sounds like a large choir singing*, I thought. It had been only eleven weeks since our country was shocked by the events of 9/11. Patriotism ran high.

Next, Stephen warmly introduced me, and I entered the stage to audience applause. *This is what you were put on the planet to do*, a voice whispered in my head, reminding me of my purpose.

Standing in front of these young, talented musicians, I again thanked God for how He had guided my steps to this place, where I not only had the best view in the house, but I could also touch hearts through the gift of music.

I raised my baton and conducted from my heart, as the music of "Rachel's Song" poured out of every part of the stage. When we finished, the audience honored me with a standing ovation—to which I bowed in gratitude before turning with a sweeping wave of appreciation to the orchestra.

After the concert, several of these young musicians confessed that they were thrilled to have me present as a living, breathing composer—conducting my own work.

Warming hearts with my music never grows old.

Creating Music for Another
UNC-TV Program

Remember the ripple I mentioned earlier? It kept expanding.

If one of my New Year's resolutions for 2002 was to do something I had never done before, I was about to get my wish. The phone rang on January 2, and it was Rob Van Camp.

"How would you like to step it up a notch and write an original music score for an entire video about North Carolina's Outer Banks?" he asked.

I wasn't as sure this time about how to answer his question as I had been when he asked me to do the music for the Blue Ridge Parkway video. Some real doubts started going through my mind. *I've never done anything like this before*, I thought. *I mean, writing music for a movie or video scene is quite a bit different from writing a standalone song.*

Sensing my hesitation, Rob said that he had been talking with Evan Richey, a Julliard-trained cellist in Winston-Salem, about possibly collaborating with me on this project.

"Before I give you an answer, let me talk to Evan," I said. I did not know Evan personally, but I knew his very musical family. Evan's mother had served as the first chair for the Winston-Salem Symphony and was the concertmaster for the symphonic premier of "Rachel's Song."

I called Evan, and we arranged to meet at the WFDD-FM station on the campus of Wake Forest University where he worked part-time. I walked into the studio where Evan was working and introduced myself.

Evan is tall and stood well above me. He had a quick, friendly smile and resonant voice. *Great radio voice*, I immediately thought.

Evan and I hit it off right from the start. I liked him from the first minute we met. His confidence that we could do this project removed all my doubts. When I heard how skillful he was at playing his cello—as well as writing and arranging music—any remaining questions were answered.

We wasted no time calling Rob from the studio and telling him that we would do the project. That's when my education and appreciation for music scoring for movies began.

The next day, Evan and I went to Rob's studio. We found that Rob had already completed all the filming—as well as the tedious and time-consuming task of editing the video clips. Once again, Rob had gotten David Holt to narrate as he'd done on the Blue Ridge Parkway video.

"I'd love to show you the video," Rob told Evan and me.

We spent several hours carefully watching, minute-by-minute and sometimes frame-by-frame, marking and timing the spots where Rob wanted the music to be placed—15 seconds here, 35 seconds there, 95 seconds under narration, intro music, credits music. Evan and I made detailed notes about each clip—what the visual scene was, what the mood needed to be, what the narrator was describing, etc. The scenery was unbelievably beautiful and in high definition (720p HD). Rob's work gave us all the inspiration we needed.

Evan's studies at Julliard had prepared him well for cello performance, and writing music for synchronization to film or video was not as new to him as it was to me. My inexperience, however, did not deter us.

"We can do this," I told Evan. At this point, my own experience gave me confidence that most strong ideas could come to fruition—with hard work and divine intervention!

"Absolutely," he nodded. "We can do this."

We went back to the WFDD studios at Wake Forest University to map out our plan, which included the agreement that we would write several brand-new songs. We decided we would each come up with our own compositions, and then we would collaborate on the arrangements. Evan already had begun drafting a couple of songs that he thought would work, and I already had the beginning few measures of the title song, "The Outer Banks."

"What do you think about using some of my existing instrumental songs from my original composition albums?" I suggested. "Since I already have the piano sheet music for those albums, it would be easier for me to develop new arrangements based on those songs."

"Sure," Evan agreed. "Let's arrange them so I can play the melody on the cello, while you play the piano."

"It sounds like we have a good plan," I said. "Now all we have to do is get busy writing some new songs."

Back home, in the quietness of our empty house—Linda was in Washington, DC, during the week—I sat down at my Steinway grand piano with my pad of blank music manuscript paper and pencil on the music stand.

I closed my eyes and replayed in my mind the beautiful, colorful scenery and sounds of North Carolina's Outer Banks—the blue ocean waves rhythmically reaching into the white sandy beach, carefree children laughing as they rolled down sand dunes, families creating sand castles, the majesty beauty and attraction of the tall, slender lighthouses, the constant ocean breeze lifting colorful kites against the Carolina blue sky, the sudden plunge of a pelican diving into the water for its next meal, the painted sky sunrises and sunsets reflected in the pools of water on the beach.

I opened my eyes and placed my hands on the piano keys. I played just one note. I listened intently as the sound gradually faded away.

I opened my eyes and placed my hands on the piano keys. I played just one note. I listened intently as the sound gradually faded away.

What do I hear next? I silently asked. Then I played what I heard, another note, letting each note lead to the next, and so on.

What chords go with that phrase? I asked myself. *Is it a minor key—sad, pensive, mysterious?* No, maybe its cheerful, more upbeat in a major key. I played the phrase again, this time with some chords in the left hand.

I imagined the melody being played on Evan's cello. *Yes, I like it,* I said to myself. I wrote the melody and chords on a piece of manuscript paper. *This can be the theme song for the video, "The Outer Banks,"* I said to myself—and it was.

Evan and I met nearly every day at WFDD to work on our music, both showing up with musical manuscripts in hand. The tiny studio was barely large enough for the electronic keyboard, with a place for Evan to sit close to me with his cello. But it created magic. Evan's tone, expression, and controlled vibrato on his instrument melded perfectly with the notes and chords I played on the keyboard.

The two of us got lost in the music. Those hours with Evan in the studio became the highlight of each day. And Evan's songwriting was as brilliant as his playing. Evan's song, "Jockey's Ridge," is still a favorite of mine. He wrote this song, performed the piano and keyboard parts, and sang the vocals. The song was jazzed up a notch when Evan's friend, Patrick Tucker, added some breathtaking jazz fills on his flugelhorn. "Jockey's Ridge" later became a frequently played song on a Sunday Jazz Brunch radio program in Bethesda, Maryland.

By early February, we had fifteen songs done and delivered to Rob for him to edit into the video. On March 2 of that year, the completed video was first broadcast on UNC-TV during their telethon fundraiser across North Carolina. The people calling in with donations gave the entire production high praise. *The Outer Banks: North Carolina's Coastal Treasure* was broadcast many times.

Evan and I liked the music we created so much that we decided to release it on a CD. We released our original songs in April, and the music sold briskly. As a way of promoting the CD, Evan and I did a four-hour personal appearance and performance on April 13 at a local gift shop called Salem Creek. We set up our place to play on the balcony upstairs and enjoyed filling the whole store with music. We met many happy customers who were very delighted by the music.

It doesn't get much better than this, I told myself after spending a day immersed in music.

I didn't know it then, but right around the corner, I'd face another threshold moment where I had a choice to make.

Would I make the right one?

CHAPTER EIGHTEEN

Never a Dull Moment

"I know that God gives special people a priceless talent and some of us the ability to cherish and enjoy that talent."
~MADELYN

A few years earlier, I needed to choose between AT&T and pursuing music full time. I chose music. And that was one of the best decisions I ever made. Following this dream allowed me to create even more heartwarming music.

Serving as my own boss also gave me the flexibility I needed to help Linda care for her parents. I didn't need to request time off or worry about putting a colleague in a bind while attending to family matters. Instead, I managed my own schedule and did what I needed to do.

After Linda's parents eventually passed away in 1999, she and I had settled into a routine with Combs Music in North Carolina. I continued to write, record, and distribute music, and we had some much-needed downtime. But that would soon change—again.

In November 2001, just after 9/11, Linda was recruited and took a position with the EPA in Washington. Once again, we had long weeks apart while she worked in DC and returned to North Carolina for the weekends. By spring of 2002, we decided that I would spend weekdays in DC with her, and then we'd both return to North Carolina on weekends. *At least that way we will be together*, I thought.

But that didn't mean I was done with music! To keep Combs Music going in my absence, I formed a management agreement with Drew and Marlene Parker, the owners of Separk Music in Winston-Salem. They were great wholesale customers of Combs Music and had become close friends. In my absence, Separk Music assumed all of Combs Music's fulfillment responsibilities for wholesale and retail orders, an arrangement that worked well for both parties.

With my background in information technology (IT), I found a job working in the Department of Agriculture Rural Utilities Services (RUS) organization, headed by a wonderful leader from Kentucky, Hilda Legg. Over the next five years, my responsibilities kept increasing. When my friend and colleague, Scott Charbo, was asked by President Bush to move over to the new Homeland Security Department as their chief information officer (CIO), I was appointed by the President to take Scott's place as the USDA chief

1 knew this would be a demanding role, but I was ready for the challenge.

information officer—in charge of IT for the entire department. With over twenty-five agencies and more than 100,000 employees worldwide, the USDA was a huge organization. As CIO, I had responsibility for more than 1,000 IT personnel—with a budget of over $2 billion. I knew this would be a demanding role, but I was ready for the challenge.

When I went to the USDA, I had no reason to think that my music could play a role in this vast organization. The executive leadership team for USDA turned out to be a close-knit team with regular, after-hours meetings every Thursday in the Williamsburg Room. We all sat around the historic conference table that had been used by President Reagan and the six other leaders of the world's largest developed economies in the historic ninth G7 Summit in 1983, in Williamsburg, Virginia. *What an honor!* I couldn't help but picture those world leaders there, in the same seats where we conducted our business.

It didn't take long before I got to know my colleagues personally. As they learned about my music, I shared some of my music CDs with them. "Rachel's Song" became the favorite song for Deputy Secretary Jim Moseley, among others.

My reputation for my piano music became widely known throughout the USDA. When it came time for the annual talent show in November, which raised charitable contributions for the Combined Federal Campaign (CFC), the organizers invited me to be one of the performers. Why not? I thought, never anticipating that my two worlds would overlap.

On Wednesday morning, November 20, 2002, all of the performers and I gathered back in the relatively small greenroom behind the stage of

Jefferson Auditorium in the USDA South Building. As I looked around the room, I felt the nervous energy. We all wanted to give our best performances in front of our peers and leaders—and their families—as well as other invited guests and coworkers who had purchased tickets. Front and center would be Secretary of Agriculture Ann Veneman, alongside Deputy Secretary Jim Moseley and a host of Under Secretaries of the numerous USDA agencies.

As my own nerves kept me moving, I stepped out to the side of the stage and peeked around the curtain. The auditorium seated nearly 500 people, and it was almost full. I spotted and waved to Linda sitting in the front row in her reserved seat, along with the USDA executive leadership team. The event was sold out.

At 10:00 a.m. sharp, Master of Ceremonies Claiborn Crain introduced our first performer, Barbara Smith. Barbara beautifully sang "The Star-Spangled Banner" as the audience stood and sang along. From the TV monitor in the greenroom, those of us waiting to perform sang along as well. Each vocal performer sang to professional accompaniment tracks, and each one received rousing applause upon finishing. I must say that my favorite singer was Carmen Humphrey who sang "Saving All My Love for You." If you closed your eyes and didn't know it, you would swear that it was Whitney Houston singing—with her strong-yet-sweet vocal chords hitting each note perfectly.

The performer right before me beautifully sang an inspiring song by Yolanda Adams called "Never Give Up." The audience loved it. We walked past each other on the stage, doing a mid-stage high-five, as I entered with her departure.

Looking out into the dimly lit auditorium, I saw Linda giving me her most encouraging smile. I took a deep breath, said a short prayer—*Lord, help me do my best*—sat down at the piano, and began to play "Rachel's Song"—as I had done hundreds of times before.

The amplified piano music reverberated throughout the auditorium. As the sound bounced back, I loved the tone. The longer I played, the tension and anxiety totally left me. I concluded the song as I always do—playing the final arpeggio chord up on the highest notes of the piano, simultaneously with a D flat octave on the lowest notes on the piano. I held those final notes as long as they sounded, then raised my foot from the sustain pedal.

Only then did I look to the audience, as they loudly applauded. I stood up, took a slow bow, and walked off the stage to the greenroom. Everyone in the room greeted me with encouraging accolades and congratulations. I felt joyful and satisfied—not only at my performance—but that I could do work that I loved, with music still at my fingertips, literally.

At the end of the show, the entire cast came onstage to lead the singing of "America the Beautiful"—with me accompanying on the piano. The audience eagerly shared their voices with gusto. Our hour-and-a-half program proved a rousing success for a good cause.

Retirement 2.0

By the summer of 2007, Linda and I decided the time had come for us to leave Washington once again and return to life in North Carolina. I resigned as the CIO of the USDA at the end of June, and Linda left her position as Controller of the United States at the end of August.

After we left, Linda received an invitation from President George W. Bush for both of us to return to the White House for a private meeting with him in the Oval Office. Of course we accepted!

At the time of our appointment, the two of us walked to the White House Northwest Appointment Gate on Pennsylvania Avenue and presented our IDs to the Secret Service inside the small guard house. After the security system showed that we were cleared to enter, we received our visitors' badges and began making our way up the walkway toward the West Wing visitors' entrance. On our right, we walked past the area where the national media set up TV cameras for those "live from the White House" news reports, with the White House in the background.

The scene could have felt surreal to me, except that it wasn't the first time I'd been in situations that felt like a dream. I was beginning to accept that my reality was often greater than I could have imagined—as God blessed us with these once-in-a-lifetime opportunities more than once! Not to mention, this was familiar territory to Linda, as her career of public service in Washington, DC, had placed her very close to our nation's leaders, including three Presidents.

As we approached the West Wing visitors' entrance, we saw the US Marine sentry standing guard to the right of the double doors, signifying that the President was in the West Wing. The Marine sentry snapped to attention, did a right face, and opened the door for us as we walked into the foyer and through another door into the lobby. Immediately on our right was a Secret Service uniformed agent sitting behind a desk. We were warmly welcomed, and our credentials were again checked on the computer. Then we were invited to enjoy the artwork and historic furnishings in the lobby or take a seat on a meticulously upholstered, blue camelback sofa while we waited.

Shortly before our appointment time, a special assistant to President Bush entered the lobby. She said, "President Bush is ready to see you now. Please follow me."

Before we sat down, Linda and I both looked above the sofa and admired the beautifully framed, famous painting by Emanuel Leutze of George Washington crossing the Delaware. We learned that this original painting was the smallest of three versions that Leutze had painted.

Shortly before our appointment time, a special assistant to President Bush entered the lobby. She said, "President Bush is ready to see you now. Please follow me."

As we entered the short hallway, the special assistant pointed out that through the open doorway immediately on our right was the Roosevelt Room. We caught sight of the long conference table surrounded by sixteen comfortable looking chairs upholstered in light brown leather. The back of one chair was taller than all the others—that one was reserved for the President.

At the end of the short hallway, we went through a door into another hallway. The special assistant guided us to the right. The first door on our left led to the Cabinet Room, and the next door led to the President's secretary. My anticipation rose as we got closer to the Oval Office.

Linda was cool as a cucumber. She had met with President Bush several times. She was in familiar territory.

We could see the open door on the left to the Oval Office, where a member of the Secret Service stood. As we entered the Oval Office, President Bush was already standing behind the historic Resolute Desk, ready to greet us.

"Mr. President, Dr. Linda Combs and her husband, Dave, are here to see you," the special assistant announced.

President Bush walked toward us with a big smile on his face, shook hands with both of us, and said, "Welcome to the Oval Office." His down-to-earth, Texas accent and friendly personality put us at ease immediately.

"Linda," he started, "I want to thank you so much for your years at the EPA, DOT, and OMB as controller of the United States." He spoke in detail that demonstrated to me that he truly knew Linda's accomplishments and appreciated her work. Turning to me, he said, "Dave, thank you for your service at the USDA. I have many friends at the USDA who speak highly of you—both personally and professionally," he said.

"Thank you for your leadership, Mr. President," I told him.

"It was a privilege to work for you," Linda added.

After a brief talk, the President wished us well as we returned home to North Carolina. A White House photographer entered the room and invited us to have our photo taken with the President to memorialize the occasion.

Our time with President Bush may have lasted only ten minutes, but it was long enough to make a lasting memory for Linda and me. No, I didn't get to play "Rachel's Song" for President Bush, but I believe that moments like these provided creativity and inspiration for my ongoing music compositions.

Symphony of the Mountains Performs "Rachel's Song"

Beginning in 1987, the Blowing Rock, North Carolina, Chamber of Commerce sponsored an annual patriotic "Symphony by the Lake" event in July at the Chetola Resort. Linda and I had attended this festive occasion many times. We were impressed with the performance of the Symphony of the Mountains orchestra from Kingsport, Tennessee, conducted by Cornelia Laemmli Orth, when we heard them in 2012. Cornelia charmed and engaged each member of the audience in such a personal way, I think every person felt like they sat with her one-on-one during the concert.

In July of 2013, the same orchestra performed "Rachel's Song" at all three of their summer concerts—Chetola Resort, Blowing Rock, North Carolina; UVA-Wise, Wise, Virginia; and Allandale Mansion in Kingsport, Tennessee. Linda and I attended the performances at Blowing Rock and Kingsport. We were able to take my ninety-four-year-old mother to the Kingsport performance. Mama's mind was very sharp, but her mobility was limited. What made that performance so special to me is that it was the only time Mama ever heard my music performed—other than me privately playing it for her on the piano. She was really honored to be there and hear and fully appreciate the performance. By the big smile on her face, I could sense the pride that she felt when I was recognized by Cornelia as the composer. Mama passed away three-and-a-half years after this concert. A video of this Symphony of the Mountains performance is on my YouTube channel (combsmusic). Scan this QR code to go to the YouTube video.

Ninetieth Anniversary Homecoming at Calvary Baptist Church in Erwin

Calvary Baptist Church in Erwin, Tennessee, was celebrating their ninety-year anniversary on Sunday, June 22, 2014. Former pastors, ministers of music, and members were all invited to a special worship service. I was invited to perform "Rachel's Song" for the offertory meditation.

Linda and I drove to Erwin on Saturday and spent the night in Mama's house. It seemed strange to be there without her, but we knew she was being well taken care of at a rehab center in Winston-Salem. We got up early Sunday morning and put on our casual clothes.

There was no food in the house, since the refrigerator had been totally emptied. No problem, I thought as we headed to Huddle House restaurant for a good breakfast. We had plenty of time, since the church service didn't start until 11:00 a.m. When we got back from breakfast, I got my clothes bag out of the closet where I had hung it up and unzipped it. Inside were my navy sport coat, dress shirt, and tie.

And no pants!

What?! Not again! I chided myself. Unfortunately, I had pulled this stunt once before on a trip to Boiling Springs, North Carolina, for a banquet at Gardner Webb University.

Now what? I thought. The only other pants I had were the Bermuda shorts that I'd worn on the way over.

"It's Sunday morning. Where are we going to get a pair of pants on Sunday?" I asked Linda.

"Walmart!" we both exclaimed at the same time.

Our only hope rested in the Walmart ten minutes away. *But will they have any pants that would both fit me and look decent with my navy sports coat?* I wondered.

We sped off to Walmart and practically ran to the men's pants area. After the two of us scanned every nook and cranny of the department, we found a pair of khaki pants. They weren't exactly dress pants, but I believed they were close enough that nobody would notice. Racing back to the house, I threw on my clothes, ran out the door, and we raced to the church.

As we entered church, I spoke with so many people that I hadn't seen in a long time—people who were an important part of my youth, like the daughters of Preacher Green, my good friend and classmate Bruce Grubb, and former choir members Joyce Miller, and Buck and Jean Foster.

Linda and I were seated near the front of the sanctuary on the left side close to the piano. While the offertory prayer was given, I quietly rose from my seat and made my way toward the Steinway grand piano. My thoughts raced back to memories of the first time I played this very piano for church fifty years before as a nervous teenager. I thought, *today is the first time that I will play this piano without my late music mentor, Doris Miller, playing with me on the organ.* I could feel a lump in my throat as my emotions welled up within me.

Before I sat down to play, I could not pass up the opportunity to say a few words of gratitude to the many people present who meant so much to my life. As I stood by the piano, I choked up while also paying tribute to the dozens of dear people who had passed on, like Preacher and Mrs. Green, Doris Miller, and others. I could tell by the tearful expressions on others' faces that they felt the same way.

It was time to begin playing "Rachel's Song." The feel and sound of that piano in that sanctuary felt like being embraced by an old friend. As I finished playing, I experienced the same familiar emotions that I had so many times before in this church—feelings that the music had deeply touched the hearts and souls of everyone present, including me.

The entire worship service that day moved me so deeply that I no longer thought about my new Walmart pants.

CHAPTER NINETEEN

IS THERE A SONG INSIDE OF YOU?

"'Rachel's Song' speaks to the soul, it stirs the spirit, it fills and occupies the mind with the past, the present, and the future simultaneously."
~BILL

Jim Carter's Song

About a week before Christmas in 2019, I got a call from long-time friend and Sunday school classmate, Benny Bowes. As I expected, Benny called to give me an update on our mutual friend, Jim, who had been mostly housebound for weeks dealing with issues of pain, weakness, and loss of appetite—not to mention grieving over the loss of his wife just four months earlier. Benny and I had been looking for a good way to cheer up Jim—taking his mind off his troubles.

"Hey Dave, I think Jim is finally feeling well enough to get out of the house for a little while. How does this Friday look for you? If you're free, I'd love to pick up Jim and head over to your house for lunch and a game of pool. I think it would do him some good," he said.

"That works for me, Benny. Looking forward to it." I always enjoyed catching up with old friends, and I hoped we could encourage Jim.

"Great! I'll pick up Jim and some BBQ from our favorite restaurant, Real Q, and we'll be at your house around one o'clock," Benny told me before we said our goodbyes.

I was already downstairs waiting for Benny and Jim when they arrived that Friday afternoon with the BBQ.

"Hey friends," I greeted them both warmly with handshakes and hugs. "Do you like the beautiful day I requested just for the two of you?" I pointed at the large windows lining the outside walls of our finished basement as the sunlight pierced the bluest of skies.

Jim was as cheerful and upbeat as always, never one to complain. I couldn't help but notice that he had lost a lot of weight. And he was walking a little slower.

Linda delivered a big pitcher of sweet tea to help us wash down the BBQ sandwiches, potato chips, and hush puppies. While we ate, we caught up.

"Jim," I told him in between bites, "I want you to know how happy I am to see you. Do you have any idea how much I've missed you?" I spoke from my heart.

"Thanks for that, Dave," Jim replied. "Have I told you how happy I am to be outside of my house?" he asked as we all shared a laugh.

As we ate and caught up, the conversation turned to music.

"You know how much Edith and I always loved hearing you play 'Rachel's Song,'" Jim said as sadness crept into his eyes. It had only been four months since he lost his dear wife, and her memorial service was still fresh in our minds and heavy on our hearts.

What Jim said next caught Benny and me by surprise.

"Did I tell you I made up a song of my own many years ago?" Jim asked. "It's just a simple tune that has stayed with me all these years." He smiled for a moment before continuing. "Funny, I've never told anybody about it."

"Does it have any words?" Benny asked.

"No. No words," Jim responded. "Just the tune."

"Well, I'd love to hear it. Could you hum the song for us?" I asked.

He nodded and said, "Wait a minute." Jim paused for a few seconds. We could see that he was thinking of how to start the song. Then he said "Yeah," and began singing the melody with just the word "da."

"Da da da da, da da, da da—da da da da da…"

I realize that reading the letters *da da da* on a page don't give you much of an idea of what it sounded like. But as someone with a musical ear, I can say that I was amazed at what I heard! His simple, catchy tune had a great song structure—beginning, middle part, and ending—and I loved it.

"Jim, you came up with such a beautiful tune!" I told him sincerely.

"Thanks," Jim answered as he shrugged. "But I can't find them. I mean the notes."

> His simple, catchy tune had a great song structure—beginning, middle part, and ending—and I loved it.

"You already found them in your head, Jim," I told him quickly. "And I can find those notes on the piano and write your song down for you."

"That would be great," Jim said gratefully with a big smile.

"Your song has a great structure in terms of the melody line, the rhythm pattern, and the chord progression," I told him.

"The only musical instrument I play is the radio," Jim laughed. "So, what you just said means nothing to me."

"That's okay," I said. "The important thing is that you came up with something magnificent. It's your song, it sounds good to you, and it means something to you. You don't have to know music to write a great song. And I think it is really great."

Jim smiled, clearly satisfied with the feedback. Then Jim, the retired business accountant, showed Benny and me his analytical side.

"The more songs I hear and try to copy on the piano, the more I realize it doesn't take a whole lot of notes to create a song. I mean 'Blessed Assurance' has just nine notes. And then it just repeats over and over," Jim said, demonstrating what made him such a highly successful businessman. He had counted the notes or beats in the song. And he was right. The first phrase of "Blessed Assurance" does begin with nine notes.

After eating lunch, Jim and I shifted to a pool game.

"What game would you like to play?" I asked.

"Eight-ball is fine," he immediately responded as he carefully picked out his desired cue stick from the rack on the wall.

This is going to be interesting, I thought to myself. *I believe that Jim has played pool before.*

I was right. Jim was a phenomenal pool player, the kind that lined up his next shot before taking his current one. While Jim started to run the table, Benny cheered him on. While we had such a great time and let our competitive natures show, what I remember most vividly is how Jim seemed to forget about his pain for those minutes and just lose himself in the games. Sure, he had to sit down periodically and rest, but when it was his turn, he was at the table planning and taking his shots.

When it was time to leave, Jim thanked Benny and me for our special gift of friendship and giving him such an enjoyable afternoon.

As the three of us hugged, Benny and I told Jim that the pleasure was all ours. Deep down I prayed that this would not be the last time we would see each other.

That night, Benny sent me a message that mirrored the joy I had experienced in the company of my dear friends.

"The smiles and joy you created…will be remembered for many days to come. It was exciting to witness Jim's old youthful pool skills come to life and at least give you a challenge," Benny wrote.

The next morning, I woke up with Jim's tune on my mind. I wasted no time sitting down at the piano and writing out the lead sheet. Then I made a recording on my iPhone of me playing Jim's song on my Kurzweil synthesizer. By 3:00 p.m. that day, I emailed my recording and the written-out notes to Jim.

"What can I say except thank you," Jim wrote me back with his usual humble spirit. "I did not expect you to do all of this, especially the sheet music. While 'Jim's Song' will never make the top forty, you've given me something concrete to use for improvement if I want to." He then added, "Also, thank you and Linda for my first fun day in several months.… I hope Benny doesn't go nuts with *da-da-da* today!" he said, meaning that Benny might get the tune stuck in his head with the way Jim had sung it.

Turns out that Benny and I both got the tune stuck in our heads.

Jim's message confirmed my feeling that he didn't fully know how important his little song could be, not just to him, but to his family for generations to come. But I felt good that I was able to take it out of his head and out in the open for all of them to hear and enjoy.

Only two weeks later, I got word from Benny that Jim's condition had been diagnosed as stage 4 cancer. His two daughters were taking care of him at home. His son, Jamie, and his family who lived in California would fly into North Carolina as soon as they could.

My heart broke for Jim and his family. *What else can I do?* I wondered.

On January 14, I had an idea and reached out to Gary Prim in Nashville.

"Hi Gary, this is Dave," I told him. "I have a situation here on my end, and I wonder if I could ask a huge favor from you," I said as I explained Jim's prognosis and my desire to have the song arranged and recorded as soon as possible for the family.

Gary told me that he would do it as soon as possible, but he also explained that he was booked solid in recording sessions.

"But I promise you that I will work on this as quickly as possible," he assured me.

Benny called me on Friday morning, January 17, to let me know that Jim was slipping in and out of consciousness. The doctors didn't know how much longer he would last. I so wanted Jim to hear Gary Prim's version of his song that I called Gary as soon as I got off the phone. Unfortunately, Gary was in the middle of a recording session. I apologized for the interruption as I explained the urgent circumstances.

"Let me see what I can do," Gary said before he said goodbye.

I just knew that Gary would find a way to get it done.

Sure enough, just after 4:00 p.m., I got a message from Gary with the recording file attached. During one of the breaks, Gary had slipped away to a room with a piano and recorded Jim's song on his iPhone.

As I hit play, Gary's arrangement filled the room—stunning and unmistakably in his signature, beautiful style.

After I listened to it, I immediately sent the recording to Jim's son, Jamie (still in California), and Benny. Jamie absolutely loved it and sent word to Benny to ensure someone played it for Jim on some headphones. Still in and out of consciousness, we couldn't know if Jim would hear his song. But we had to try.

Jamie arrived from California on Sunday, January 19. He and his two sisters stayed by Jim's bedside while continuously playing Jim's song. The song still played when Jim slipped away to heaven shortly after midnight, exactly one month after our wonderful afternoon together.

At Jim's memorial service, I had the privilege to play "Jim Carter's Song." Before I played, Benny told the story of our wonderful afternoon with Jim when he introduced us to his beautiful song. As usual, I was a bit nervous as I got up to play but thinking of the joy that "Jim Carter's Song" would forever bring to his kids and grandkids got me through it.

Jim may be gone from this life, but his song will touch lives forever, I thought.

Do you have a song inside of you? If so, I humbly suggest that you consider sharing it with someone who may be able to bring it to life. Your song may just be waiting to touch others and transform your life.

CHAPTER TWENTY

MUSIC TELLS A STORY OF ITS OWN

"I first heard your 'Rachel's Song' about four or five years ago.... Honestly, the hairs on my arms stood up, and I immediately started to cry and laugh at the same time."

~SUE

There was a personal reason I felt such urgency and passion to help Jim hear the song he had carried inside his head for so many years.

Three days before Christmas in 1980—before "Rachel's Song" had come to me—Linda and I were having dinner with friends that we had not seen in a while. We had just finished eating a delicious home-cooked dinner, and our house held a blend of the sweet scents of freshly baked foods and our fresh Fraser fir Christmas tree. After cleaning up the kitchen, we descended to our bright and cheerful finished basement. Christmas music was playing and lots of laughter filled the air. My new ping pong table, situated in its special place under the lights, was practically begging to be put to use. A spirited ping-pong match began while Linda engaged in friendly catch-up conversation with our guests.

While the ping-pong battle was going full force, Linda excused herself to answer the ringing phone. She returned a moment later with a face that conveyed some concern.

"Dave," Linda told me, "it's your Uncle Paul. He wants to talk to you," she said.

Setting my paddle on the table, I walked over to the phone and greeted my daddy's brother, Uncle Paul.

"David, I've got some sad news," Uncle Paul said, his voice breaking. "Your dad was killed in a hit-and-run automobile accident tonight in Florida," he continued as his voice cracked.

It was as if time stopped, as my mind tried to process what I was hearing. My body froze. "Oh, no!" I paused, not knowing what to say next. "How did this happen?" I was so choked up, I could hardly get the words out. My heart broke instantly.

Everything blurred, and my thoughts raced to seek more facts—as if learning more could change the outcome. *A hit and run accident? Who was driving? How did it happen?* I asked myself—or Uncle Paul. My emotions fought to take over my mind, and I couldn't be sure what I was thinking—versus what I was verbalizing to him.

Uncle Paul told me that the man who called to deliver the news was driving both himself and Daddy to a hospital in Sarasota to visit a friend. While the man drove on a boulevard, a car pulled out in front of them. Daddy's friend swerved left to avoid the car, crossed the median, and ended up sideways in the oncoming lane of traffic. An oncoming car crashed directly into the passenger door—where Daddy was sitting. When the EMS arrived, they administered CPR but were unable to revive him. The car that caused the accident drove off and was never identified.

Uncle Paul had given me all the seemingly important details, yet no amount of clarity would change the reality that *Daddy was gone.*

After I hung up the phone, I tried to pull myself together to make the hardest phone call of my life—to my brother, Don. Don took the tragic news as badly as I did. We didn't find many words to say to one another. Instead we spent most of the call sobbing together. This was our first real taste of overwhelming grief. Daddy was only sixty-one years old.

I called Mama next to break the news to her. Even though she and Daddy had been divorced for thirteen years, the news hit her hard too. As she sobbed, I felt that her tears were not just for Don and me, but for Daddy, too.

That Christmas season and the days following this shocking phone call were like no other time that Linda nor I had experienced. The sudden death of my father was gut-wrenching and emotionally overwhelming. Linda and I—and my brother, Don, and his wife, Chris—spent a good part of Christmas Day on Eastern Airlines flights to get to Bradenton-

Sarasota, Florida, for the funeral. The only bright spot that day was on the last leg of our flight. Our dear friends, Jim and Louise Broyhill, happened to be on the same flight. They were very consoling to us.

On Friday morning, we met Phil Pritchard, the executor of Daddy's estate, and we all went to Daddy's house. Everything looked pretty much the same as it had the last time Linda and I visited him. Only this time, it was eerily lifeless—no music playing, no smells of cooking in the kitchen.

As we walked into the living room, Linda's eye caught a glimpse of a familiar card lying on an end table next to the sofa. It was on top of a small stack of what appeared to be recently opened mail. Linda picked the card up and saw it was her school board candidate campaign card on which she had written, "I won!" in big letters right below her picture. Linda had enclosed it with our Christmas card, also on the table. Knowing that he had gotten our Christmas card, and knew that Linda had won her election, was somehow comforting at the time.

Mr. Pritchard asked us to look around the house and take any items that we would like to have from Daddy's estate. Since most of my fondest, earliest memories of Daddy involved music, I quickly found items that connected me to him: a couple of old violins and violin cases, a couple of autoharps, and the wonderful music books that he and I had enjoyed playing together—he on the organ and I on the piano. I also knew I wanted his Hammond organ with Leslie speakers. Later Friday morning, other members of the family arrived and joined us at Daddy's house— Uncle Paul, Aunt Phyllis, and Grandma Combs. It was not how I wanted to get together, but nonetheless I was glad to see them all.

Daddy's funeral was officiated by Reverend Gerald Derstine, the founder of Christian Retreat in Bradenton, and a nationally-known TV minister and author. Daddy had supported the Christian Retreat ministry and attended many of his sermons. I mainly remember how dynamic and charismatic he was as he delivered an eloquent eulogy for Daddy. The organist and choir from Palma Sola Community Church provided the music. I couldn't tell you what songs they sang. My mind kept constantly thinking about how surreal this all seemed. I just couldn't believe that Daddy was gone at the young age of sixty-one.

The brief graveside service was held at the Palma Sola Community Church in Bradenton. It was a beautiful, old church that Daddy loved to attend. Interestingly, this historic church was first known in the late 1800s as The Church in the Wildwood, the same name as one of my daddy's favorite old songs.

After saying our final goodbyes to Daddy, cherished family members, and friends, Linda, and I returned to North Carolina. A short time after we got home, I was feeling a bit lost, so I decided to keep myself busy by tuning my 100-year-old Knabe baby grand piano. As part of a practice I'd followed for years, after tuning the piano, I placed my fingers on the keys and played, so I could hear the beautiful sounds of the instrument.

I started in the key of C. Even before I struck the next note, I seemed to hear the chord progression playing inside my head. My fingers flowed naturally, as if they knew where to go on their own. Although I didn't think about it at the time, I now believe that I was experiencing true inspiration from God.

I missed Daddy dearly, yet I knew that I would see him again someday. Instead of spending Christmas at home with loved ones, I had spent the holidays saying goodbye to the man who lovingly held me, as a small boy, on his lap as we played piano together.

The tune that came out of my fingers that day in January of 1981 revealed my feelings better than any words could express. My feelings became sounds; my heart became music. Full of both melancholy and happy memories—and some sadness mixed with hope—that evening God gave me a tune that would change the course of my life.

"Rachel's Song" came to me as I processed the loss of my daddy. Years later, by dedicating this song to a precious infant named Rachel on her Christening day, I set the song free to touch as many lives as possible. In some way, it was as if my daddy lived on—as the song was dedicated to this new life. It also gave me *new* life—and the passion to pursue sharing the song with the world, while building Combs Music.

Just as I owed the start of my music passion to my daddy, I felt I owed some of my inspiration for this song to him as well.

Music never ends; it lives on forever.

WHAT OTHERS ARE SAYING ABOUT THIS MUSIC

"There is no doubt in my mind that this music is indeed inspired."
~SHIRLEY

Thank You for Telling Me Your Stories

Over the years, I have continued to realize what a blessing it was for me to receive this beautiful, peaceful melody—made up of this special combination of notes and chords. I've realized what a privilege it is to share this special gift of music with the world. Just as this song was received and written down note-by-note by me (with God's inspiration orchestrating my hand and ear), every letter, word, and sentence that people have put on paper and written to me about this melody continues to demonstrate the power and beauty of this gift.

I wish to conclude *Touched by the Music* by sharing a sampling from the inspiring notes I've received through the years from people who have been blessed by my music. To respect the privacy of the writers, these are not necessarily word-for-word notes or letters, but rather the essence of a selected few of the over 50,000 notes, emails, and letters I've received. It would be great to include them all, but that would be more than enough for an entire book on its own.

If you play "Rachel's Song" in the background and read these inspirational words and thoughts, I believe you'll get a glimpse into the beautiful world of peace and purity that I experienced when God first gave me this melody. You will be blessed as you learn from others' stories, the many ways they were touched while listening to this music.

My hope is that, like the 50,000 people who wrote me, you too will be touched by the music. And if you are, I hope that you will share it with someone else who needs it.

Selected Special Notes and Stories from People Who Were Touched by the Music

"Not so long ago, I became an EMT. Two months ago, on our way out for dinner, my husband and I saw an old man fall backward on the sidewalk clutching his chest. All I could think as I ran was that I never wanted to really use the CPR I'd learned. The gentleman was okay but breathing much too fast out of fear. From my husband's car radio, 'Rachel's Song' was playing. I didn't know of you then, but I yelled to turn that music up loud, and I comforted the old man by having him listen to the heavenly lullaby-like song. By the time it finished, he was so calm, and a doctor had come from a nearby office to further care for him. The next day I spent an hour tracking your song down from the radio station and then ordered all the tapes you've done. You'll probably get orders from a few of my friends too, as in my enthusiasm, I've managed to permeate our squad house and my car with your talent. Please keep up your most appreciated work and don't ever be discouraged—it's beautiful."

~CAROL

"I have listened to 'Rachel's Song' over and over again. I am a newly recovering alcoholic, and your music was suggested to me because of my extreme restlessness. The first time I listened to it through a headset and peacefully fell asleep. I continued to do so until about four months ago. A member of my AA group asked if she could borrow my tapes. She never returned them. About a month later, I went out and purchased the tapes once again—and slept soundly and with a great deal of peace once again. It still amazes me the extent your music affects me, especially emotionally. Tears swell constantly. I continuously enjoy your music. It has truly helped me maintain my peacefulness, and in doing so, has helped me maintain my sobriety. Thank you for sharing your music and talent. Your music has touched parts of my heart and soul that I believed to be long dead. Once again, thank you for helping make a difference in my life. May God bless you always. Sincerely and gratefully…"

~JOAN

"Thank you so much for composing and recording 'Rachel's Song.' When I first heard it, it completely engulfed me. I've now played it for many friends. One of my friends goes to sleep with your music. My husband says, 'I'd like to go to heaven with that song.'"

~GAIL

"I have been listening to 'Rachel's Song' since I purchased it yesterday. In all honesty, I have never heard anything more beautiful. As a Christian, there is no doubt in my mind that this music is indeed inspired. Before reading the story behind 'Rachel's Song,' my mind immediately took off with the story of Jacob, Rachel, and Leah. This music gives me tranquil moments, as my mind thinks on Him whom my heart loves, the Lord Jesus. I am thankful indeed to have your music. It makes my heart sing and allows me to put thoughts and feelings of my own to it. Actually, I'm weary of so many words today; I love the quiet. Thank you. May the Lord bless you and keep you and make His face to shine upon you and give you His peace. With appreciation..."

~SHIRLEY

"I just want to thank you for giving me such wonderfully inspiring music. The first time I heard your music I was enchanted from beat one. Nothing had ever filled me with such emotion. I felt like I was floating between the clouds. I've never been touch by music quite like this before. This is the most relaxing, sensual, yet powerful music I've ever heard. I can't stop listening...."

~JENNIFER

"I have never enjoyed a tape so much as 'Rachel's Song.' So relaxing, so beautiful. I first heard it and bought it on the spot. I thought it was the most beautiful piece I'd ever heard, and I still do. I took the tape to work, and my boss loved it just as much as I. He plays it all the time. It turned into him my borrowing my own tape! I bought another one of your tapes this past weekend. My boss will never know, and I now have one all my

own. Thanks so much for beautiful music. When someone does something for the enjoyment of other people, they should be commended."
~PATRICIA

"I have your disk of 'Rachel's Song' and have almost worn it out already! I absolutely love it and find all your songs on the disk absolutely inspiring! You have a real gift of talent from God—your music is so special. It spoke to my soul. Thank you so much."
~CARROLL

"I recently had the pleasure of being introduced to your music. I purchased a tape of 'Rachel's Song' and have since warmed the hearts of my patients with it. You see, I am a nurse working with chronic and terminal patients. I play it over and over for them while on duty. It truly brings a sense of comfort and relaxation. Thank you."
~DEBRA

"I am by no means a musical genius. In fact, on a scale from one to ten, I probably fall a wee bit above zero. Fortunately, it doesn't take a musical genius to appreciate a beautiful piece of music. 'Rachel's Song' has tugged at my emotions and tear ducts for years. I can only describe this melody as beautiful. Perhaps if I were a talented writer, I could better choose a word, which would describe its haunting refrain. An artist captures a beauty on the canvas; you capture beauty through your heart, and each time I hear 'Rachel's Song' the emotional picture I create is always different. Thank you for giving me such a poignant piece of music, which touched my heart long before I knew the story behind 'Rachel's Song.' Respectfully...."
~CAROL

"We have truly worn out 'Rachel's Song.' We listen to it or one of your other tapes every single evening while lying in bed, talking about things that went on that day, cuddling, and.... Your tapes are so relaxing and soothing to the soul. God has truly used your talents in composing to make the most beautiful music we have ever listened to. As we used 'Rachel's Song' in our wedding repertoire and played it continually while on our honeymoon, it has a very special place in our hearts. Brings back those memories and feelings every time we hear that music. That's why we like to play it all the time—we love that newlywed feeling!"

~ANTOINETTE

"'Rachel's Song' is one of the most exquisitely touching pieces of music I've ever heard. Thank you for making it available. I am a psychotherapist and work a lot with wounded souls and broken hearts. 'Rachel's Song' helps me stay present and in touch—while creating a safe and nurturing space for whatever needs to happen for clients. 'Rachel's Song' is played, enjoyed, and savored daily. It feeds my own soul. I am most grateful. Blessings…."

~ELIZABETH

"Please let me tell you our story. For the last three years, my husband and I have gone through extensive infertility treatments, which concluded with the adoption of our beautiful, little daughter. We always knew we would name our daughter Rachel. Rachel was baptized this Sunday, and her godmother gave her your recording of 'Rachel's Song.' It brought tears to all of our eyes, and we play it every night as Rachel slips off to sleep. It was the most perfect gift!! Thank you so much for making the arrival of our Rachel even more special with your beautiful composition. Fondly…."

~BARBARA

"Help!!!! My wife is driving me crazy. She heard a CD titled Rachel's Song. Your company name and address were on the cover. Can you help?"

~RICK

"I first heard your 'Rachel's Song' about four or five years ago while driving to work one winter morning. I just happened to be switching radio stations and came across this piece playing. Honestly, the hairs on my arms stood up, and I immediately started to cry and laugh at the same time. Never have I heard such an incredibly beautiful, moving, enchanting, awesome melody."

~SUE

"Recently I graduated from nurse's school. At the graduation, my daughter's fiancé played 'Rachel's Song' for the processional. I just wanted you to know that there wasn't a dry eye in the building. After the ceremony, many of the visitors asked him the name of the music. This song has added greatly to my life. The college officials remarked that ours was one of the most beautiful ceremonies in the history of the college. I don't know how to thank you."

~KITTY

"Your music is absolutely beautiful, inspiring, and uplifting. There are a lot of great pianists and composers out there, but very very few bring sensitivity to the very essence of the music your works convey. Your music speaks to me in a very peaceful and majestic way."

~ELENA

"It was a most pleasant day in Cambria, California, when we first heard 'Rachel's Song' and were immediately mesmerized by this enthralling music. It sounded like a beautiful music box. My wife and I sat motionless, while this song completely enriched our souls as we clasped hands together with wondrous enjoyment. We were so touched by your musical creation that we purchased the tape and have been playing it since, spreading this joy to our friends and relatives. Thank you so much for the joy you have given my wife and me with your beautiful composition, 'Rachel's Song.' Your ardent admirer...."

~HAL

"Yesterday morning, I was driving to work, and on the radio was one of the most beautiful pieces of music I had ever heard. The music was full of love, gentleness, hope, and peace. As soon as I got to work, I

called the station and learned it was 'Rachel's Song.' I now have my own copy of the music. I can't tell you the feelings this piece of music brings to me. Thank you so much for sharing your talent with the world."
~ELAINE

"Some three or four years ago, I had the privilege to purchase a copy of 'Rachel's Song.' Since then, whenever I feel depressed or set upon by the pressures of life, I simply put that tape in my stereo, and I am completely at peace. Never have I heard such beautiful music. I am eternally grateful for your fine talent and the joy and peace your music brings to me. Thank you again."
~JACK

"'Rachel's Song' is the most beautiful instrumental I have ever heard. Keep up the good work. You give so many people pleasure and will be remembered for many generations. Thank you."
~RUTH

"Waiting in my car during the Christmas rush, your 'Rachel's Song' came on over my local radio station. The simplicity and beauty of your music made a memorable and pleasant occasion out of the traffic jam!"
~DIXON

"I love your style. I am not an accomplished pianist—far from it— but even I can play the simple but beautiful style you've written, and I sound pretty good for someone who just plays for my own enjoyment, and with limited talent. Your music makes me sound like I really know how to play. That's what I love about it. Plus it is very soothing, beautiful music to listen to. I really love it. Keep it up. Thanks for sharing your gift."
~SUE

"This is a commentary about 'Rachel's Song.' These are some of the thoughts that came to me as I listened to your beautiful song.

It sounds so much sound like breathing...like the breath of God....
Like a good life,
With a nice, even, steady flow of harmonies,
Changes, one chord leading into another constantly,
But never any real dissonance.
Its steady beat is just the right speed to breathe to,
IN 2, 3, 4, OUT 2,3,4.
The arpeggios, like harp strings, run smoothly,
From lower to higher, always giving an upward feeling,
Like being in touch with God,
And being lifted a little higher with each breath.
Surely, this music is of the Lord.
It seems like the perfect, soothing, happy sound to hear,
Even as one steps into eternity.
It never really seems to end,
But always leaves you waiting....
For the next note...or chord...or measure...or change...
or something....
But you know whatever it is, it will be beautiful.
It speaks of life...And death...And everything in between....
And everything after."
~A FAMILY FROM ILLINOIS

"Your beautiful music was introduced to me through a very dear friend. I wish to thank you for allowing me to lose my soul and cleanse my thoughts through the magic of your compositions. I can feel the emotions through the music—almost makes me feel as if I know you. The tapes are with me in my car as well as in the evening when I sleep. After listening or while listening to your beautiful music, my mood changes, and I feel relaxed and soothed—something I so deeply need at this particular time in my life."
~LYNN

"'Rachel's Song' is the most beautiful music I've heard in a long time. It allows the soul to feel."
~MARY

"I want to let you know how very important your music is in my life! In the last three years, many very special events have taken place in my life with your music playing in the background! My husband and I first heard 'Rachel's Song' in a gift shop. In fact, we were on opposite sides of a counter and came together with the same words—'Listen to that. It's beautiful!' Months later, my husband proposed marriage to me in front of the fireplace with your music playing. At our wedding, it was used as background music. Whenever we desire to be romantic, your music sets the mood."

~A FAMILY FROM CALIFORNIA

"Thank you for producing the beautiful music of your heart. Your music really helps me through the many storms in my life. Thanks for sharing your gift with me."

~WILLIAM

"I would like to let you know how much your music has ministered to my heart. I find it beautiful, peaceful, and spiritually uplifting. Thank you for using your God-given talents to minister to others. God bless you."

~LARRY

"I just wanted say thank you for the beautiful music you've brought into our home! My children and I have been through a horrible crisis, and so many days and nights your music has brought peace and relaxation into our minds and hearts. We have a lot of classical piano music, but yours is anointed with a gift that doesn't come from human abilities! Thanks for being an inspiration to my eleven-year-old son in his piano practicing as well!"

~CAROLE

"I recently received the album for 'Rachel's Song' (my first taste of your music). My soul took flight! It is truly beautiful, and you have helped make the world a better place. You have a gift, and I am truly happy for you. Congratulations and best wishes!!"

~NORMAN, NORTH CAROLINA

"Recently while in our hospital gift shop, I heard 'Rachel's Song.' I was so moved by its beauty. I gave a tape of 'Rachel's Song' to a dear lady close to us who was dying of cancer. She had played organ, piano, and accordion and loved music. Her baby grand hadn't been touched for a year, and she was waiting to die in her home when I visited. She loved the tape, and I could see her fingers playing the notes as she listened with closed eyes. She commented that the 'piece is gorgeous' and thanked me. And now, I thank you for giving all of us such beautiful music. She recently passed away, but I'm grateful to you for helping ease her pain and fears through your music. Thank you again, and I hope you'll continue to be inspired."

~JOANNE

"I am writing you in regard to the wonderful music I am enjoying frequently called 'Rachel's Song.' I have a sixteen-year-old daughter, and I already know what song I want her to come down the bridal aisle with. The melody is absolutely lovely, and your story behind 'Rachel's Song' warms my heart. The music is so touching. I too must admit, it brings a tear to my eye. Thanks for a genuinely 'heavenly' musical experience."

~SHARON

"I started listening to your music about a year ago, and of all the music that I listen to, yours is my favorite. Music is a very important part of my life, and I listen to a lot of it. I find that your music can transport me, mentally, to a lot of places in my imagination. There are also times that the same music will allow me to go about my day with a smile and better attitude, because it just makes me feel good! Then, there are the times that your music just makes me cry, but that is good! I drive our motorhome, as my husband does not like to drive, and your music is always on while I am driving. I do like to drive, and your music just makes me feel wonderful while I am going down the highway. Thank you so much for some of the most beautiful music I have ever heard!"

~BARBARA

"Absolutely beautiful music. We are round dancers and do a beautiful dance to 'Rachel's Song.' You would enjoy it."
~A FAMILY FROM MICHIGAN

"We listened to 'Rachel's Song' the whole time I was in labor with our daughter."
~A FAMILY FROM NORTH CAROLINA

"I first heard 'Rachel's Song' on our tenth anniversary trip to the Smoky Mountains where we stayed in a mountain chalet. Each time I listen to this music, I immediately recall rocking on the deck of the chalet (morning coffee in hand) feeling loved and secure, watching the mountain sunrises and beautiful mountain mist settle in the valleys, while birds sang and squirrels played in the trees around the deck. Your music is helping us cope with tremendous stress at this time. Since your music seems holy and God-graced to us, a musical prayer for the protection and happiness of mistreated babies might be the inspiration for additional work. God bless you for the comfort and repose your music provides us in our stressful moments. Your music is holy, God-graced, peaceful, instills security, provides repose."
~JODY

"I have never been so touched. In a world full of stress and daily battles, it is nice to have something that can put everything back into perspective. I would like to say thank you for composing such beautiful music. You have a true God-given talent, and you are using it to create something very beautiful. Don't ever stop."
~JO

"Approximately two months ago, I was listening to the radio and heard 'Rachel's Song.' I cannot tell you what an inspiration that was for me. I've always enjoyed piano music and have wished I could play. I'm not sure if this is a mid-life crisis (I'm an old person of forty-six) or the real thing. But after hearing your song, within a week I had a piano, and one week later I started lessons, saying, 'One day I'm going to play that song" (maybe a year down the road). 'Rachel's Song' is by far one of the most beautiful songs I have ever heard. I thank you for that."

~BONNIE

"From the first time I heard 'Rachel's Song' played on our local radio station, I fell in love with your music. Everyone who has heard your music at my house has been enraptured with it. I too had tears in my eyes the moment I heard 'Rachel's Song.' It has been played over and over. Every time I play it, it's like a new, beautiful experience to me. I will never tire of your music. Please promise me one thing: you will never stop composing music. I do not play an instrument myself, but I do love music with a passion. May your talents be enriched a hundredfold for what you have brought into the music world."

~FRANK

"I was first introduced to your talent in 1991. As your music played, I was surrounded by a calming peace. I encourage you to continue using the talent and gifts God has blessed you with. Thank you for sharing your gifts with all of us."

~SHERRY

"The first time I heard your music was in February of 1993. My twin sister and I were staying at a friend's townhouse in Scottsdale, Arizona. She had your disc on her beautiful sound system along with four other discs we never heard because we just played your disc over and over. From the very first time I heard it, I said it was the closest thing to angel music I had ever heard. Thank you for hours and hours of angel music."

~BARBARA

"I bought 'Rachel's Song' in June and have not played any other in our tape deck in our truck. This is the sweetest music I have ever purchased!"

~LINDA

"I found your 'Rachel's Song' several years ago in California, and I fell in love with the music. It seemed to comfort me at a time when I was still grieving over the sudden death of my young son in an auto accident. I'm still grieving, but it is easier. I've acquired all of your releases since then, but 'Rachel's Song' remains my favorite. Your music seems to touch my inner soul and helps me feel closer to my son."
~CATHERINE

"I have received much comfort from the music of 'Rachel's Song' since losing my husband to Alzheimer's disease eight days ago."
~HELEN

"Thank you so very much for your beautiful music, which creates such an atmosphere of worship and helps us to enter into God's presence. Over and over at home and in my car, I have listened to 'Rachel's Song.' It touches me every time. I appreciate your music. It surely must be anointed of God. May He continue to create through you. Joyfully...."
~CAROL

"I want to thank you so much for your music. I am really enjoying it. My family calls your music 'Mother's blood-pressure-taker-downer music.' They know when the tapes are on, leave Mother be."
~PAT

"My husband is lying ill, and together we are enjoying your lovely music. Thank you for the tranquil times together through your music. I am giving your music to the hospice personnel, who also share this time—which could be spent in grief, but instead is spent in peace and blessing. Also, for my family and friends who are more dear at this time. We never tire of your music. Love and blessing..."
~ETHEL

"I want to thank you for your beautiful music. The first time I heard 'Rachel's Song' on the radio, I fell in love with it. I have a performer's degree in piano and love playing along with your piano books. Each of your pieces is an exquisite gem of a masterpiece! Keep up your wonderful work. The world is a better place because of you."

~SHARMAN

"I haven't forgotten how beautiful 'Rachel's Song' is. I play it all the time. God has given you a very special gift. I do know where your blessings came from. I shared 'Rachel's Song' with my daughter, and she is seriously thinking of using this beautiful music at her wedding. This music is also very inspirational. This is the most beautiful music I have ever heard. God bless you."

~THERESA

"This summer I purchased 'Rachel's Song.' It is by far my favorite tape. I compliment you folks on your music. It is very soothing. I have been in counseling. When I leave the therapist's office, I always play 'Rachel's Song' on the way home. It has a very calming effect on me. Thank you for such fine work."

~MARILYN

"Awesome! That's what your music is.... 'Rachel's Song' surely had to be given to you by God! I hope you don't mind that I'm writing this letter to you, but I just wanted to express to you what a beautiful blessing your music has been to me. Your music has literally ministered to my heart and soul. The music is so moving, it just seems to grab my heart. Even though the tears kept coming, I realized how much my body and mind were relaxing. I literally fell asleep listening to your music. I know God has inspired you to write or compose this music by the way it has ministered to me—beautiful peace truly comes through. I want to thank you for writing and sharing your music, and may God continue to bless you because of it. This music couldn't have come into my life at a more needed time. I'm going through an overwhelmingly painful and hectic time. God has reached out and touched me through your most heart-stirring music—definitely brought God's peace. Thank you, thank you. God loves you, and so do I."

~PAULA

"Your music is so reflective, so serene; it touches my heart and makes me smile."
~RICHARD

"I don't know when I have been so touched by a song. Thank you for sharing such beauty with the world."
~MARGE

"You have created some of the most beautiful piano music I have ever listened to. This past October, my four sisters and my mom went to visit our sister. One day, we headed out to a state park and enjoyed lunch at the lodge and a nice easy hike—our mother is eighty-two years young. After the hike, on our way home, we stopped at some log cabin shops close to the state park. Upon entering one shop—it was void of any other customers—the older gentleman behind the counter slipped the recording into his player. All of a sudden, the sweetest music filled his little shop. As I browsed around, the music overwhelmed me. I tried to nonchalantly wipe the tears from my eyes, when I heard a sister inquire about the music. As she did, all of us gathered around the counter, as the gentleman started to explain the music. He took one of your albums out and put in another, as he had a sister read aloud the story behind 'Rachel's Song.' Within a short time, all of us had tears running down our cheeks. We started laughing when we realized that all of us were crying. After 'Rachel's Song,' he stopped the music and inserted 'Springtime Reflections.' He told us his favorite song he wanted to play, looked at all of us crying, and with a straight face, said, 'Do you think you all can handle another song???' We all laughed and ended up buying all of your music!!"
~BECKY

"I recently purchased 'Rachel's Song' because I had heard the title song on my local radio station. I have listened many times and still cannot get through it with dry eyes. Such beautiful music, and the arrangement and presentation are incredible."
~LARRY

"I want you to know something. I am very grateful for the gift to life that you are giving. In the winter of 1991, I had a nervous breakdown, which was diagnosed as 'severe depression.' Thank God I found a good doctor, but the long road back has been a daily struggle. Please smile today as I tell you your music ('Rachel's Song' and 'Springtime Reflections') has indeed been a part of my recovery. You make me smile."
~DIANA

"Hello, my name is Rachel. I'm writing to tell you how much I love your instrumental song, 'Rachel's Song.' My parents bought it for me, and the first time I heard it, I cried. About two years ago while my family was in Cancun on vacation, I was with my older brother swimming in the ocean. I got carried out too far by the currents. I tried to fight the waves but gave up, and I began to drown. No one helped me but my brother, who pushed my body to shore on pure adrenaline. He saved my life. This song was a gift from my parents for a new beginning for me. I thank you for writing such a beautiful song."
~RACHEL

"Thank you for sharing your special gift of music with the rest of the world."
~GLORIA

"Today is my mom's birthday. But she died six weeks ago. I wanted you to know the special place your music, 'Rachel's Song,' had in her life. She discovered you in a faraway place, and it took a year and a half to find a copy of the album. When Mom did get 'Rachel's Song,' she and a friend were going through a difficult time. They both found solace in your music. Well, time heals, and she found happiness again. Your music then was a joyful sound in her house. Mom lived alone (young fifties and vibrant), and music was a large part of her life. When she was diagnosed recently with lung cancer, a lot of inspirational tapes would help her, along with instrumental ones. Despite radiation therapy, prayers, and lots of positive thinking, Mom died three-and-a-half months after her diagnosis. Her last week was spent in an ICU on a ventilator. In the beginning of the week, she would wake for short periods of time. Though she could hear for a large part of the time, she appeared to be sleeping. It was so depressing to listen to the machines beeping and the doctors whispering, so we brought in her Walkman with her favorite album, Rachel's Song. Once when she woke up, she pointed to the headphones on her pillow and smiled. We played it over and over for seven days!! Then at her funeral, the organist moved over to the piano in church and played 'Rachel's Song.' I can't thank you enough for bringing comfort to my mom, my family, and now, so often, me. Soon, I hope your music will also bring joy to me as it did so often to Mom."

~MAUREEN

"Words cannot express the pleasure your recording of 'Rachel's Song' has brought into our home. The music is so fresh, vital—yet relaxing— and full of love and warmth. Many thanks and best wishes to you."

~ANN

"I want to tell you that we have been touched ever so deeply by your music. I have never been embraced by any other music as I have 'Rachel's Song.' That melody is known as 'Rebecca's Song' to us. We heard it before Rebecca was born, and it touched us in such a sweet way that it was quite some time before I could listen to it without being moved to tears. After reading the insert that came with the album, I knew that you had done the best thing by dedicating the song to your godchild—what a beautiful gift. At our house, we dedicated all the feelings and emotions that you captured so exquisitely in that melody to our Rebecca. She knew that song. A few days before her accident, I played the tape while I held her and fed her a bottle. When she heard it, she pushed the bottle away and just looked at me and smiled and smiled. It was a moment that I will always treasure in my memories of her. I will always be able to have her close to me through the tape of 'Rachel's Song.' Thank you for recognizing your God-given talent and sharing it with the world. You've touched our lives with your music and brought sweet and bittersweet memories to us through it. On

my granddaughter's second anniversary of her birth, I will take my portable tape player to her grave and play the music—your music—for all of us, and for her. Thank you for giving us the sweetest sounds this side of heaven. With sincere appreciation..."
~REBECCA'S MOM

"My wife and I recently purchased your album, Rachel's Song. We just love the music and can't believe that our children in college also enjoy it when they are at home. It is truly music that spans the generations. Congratulations on your artistic achievements. I am a college professor, and 'Rachel's Song' is a fantastic background music for grading those exams and term papers."
~DR. SMITH

"I wish to share a special thought with you. On New Year's Day, my daughter passed away from a long battle with cancer. During all of her treatments when things got tough and hard to handle, we played 'Rachel's Song' for her, and it seemed to relax her and soften the pain. Because she loved this song so much, we requested that the funeral home play it during the visitation at the chapel. This was the first time a different procedure was requested, and now many are following the same pattern. Everyone thought it was a nice idea, and it touched so many hearts. It was a very emotional day. Thank you for composing such a beautiful song, although I cry buckets of tears every time I hear it."
~HELEN

"I have a daughter, Rachel, age seven, so 'Rachel's Song' is very special to our whole family. Rachel calls it her tape and loves it as much as my husband and me. When you can get the attention of a seven-year-old, you have accomplished major things!!"
~SHELIA

"Just a note to tell you that we bought the CD of Rachel's Song, and it is so beautiful that it brought tears to our eyes. Over and over, I play it. What a talent and a wonderful gift you have given to the world—

hours and hours of such tranquil listening music. We rave to all our friends about your music. We are 'hooked on Combs.' Thank you, Dave Combs. We love you."

~A FAMILY FROM NORTH CAROLINA

"I've always loved my 'Rachel's Song'—but now more than ever. In March of last year, my wonderful husband had a massive stroke. He is paralyzed and wheelchair bound—a resident of a nearby nursing home. After forty-seven years of marriage, I am once again alone. If it were not for beautiful music, I could not go on. When I feel myself sliding into the dumps, I immediately put on 'Rachel's Song,' and it lifts me both emotionally and spiritually. Your music is so very beautiful! 'Rachel's Song' is my very, very favorite, and now that I am finally beginning to adjust to my situation, I will begin to add to my collection and fill my empty house with your wonderful music. Don't take your time to answer. I just want you to know how important your music is to me—and many other people as well. It is much more than entertainment."

~MELLIE

"'Rachel's Song'—it speaks to the soul, it stirs the spirit, it fills and occupies the mind with the past, the present, and the future simultaneously. It invades the very heart with such a diversification of emotions that a person—so caught completely off guard and absolutely taken by surprise by what is happening to them inside—is overwhelmed and moved to tears. And so is 'Rachel's Song.' Bless you for such communication of your inspiration, and for sharing it with others. In awe and appreciation…"

~BILL

"'Rachel's Song' is my absolute favorite. I first heard your music while on retreat in August 1990. Another person on the retreat had 'Rachel's Song' with her. She thought I would like it and let me listen to it. It really touched me deeply—something that can't really be put into words. Long after listening to it, it remained in me. She had been given it as a gift. I had to wait more than a year, but I finally got my own copy of 'Rachel's Song.' It had not been forgotten. I have since given it as a gift also. It is very special. You have a beautiful gift. Peace."

~PAT

"Your music is so relaxing and full of expression. 'Rachel's Song' is my favorite, and as I listen to it, I have visions of dancing in a grand room with covered arches, glittering crystal chandeliers, while dressed so elegantly. I love the piano and would give anything to play. You are exceptionally talented, and I truly appreciate your beautiful music."

~JUSTINE

"We have enjoyed 'Rachel's Song' so much. The music ministers much peace. I am a minister and like to play 'Rachel's Song' while I study and have quiet times in prayer. Whether or not you knew Jesus would use your music to bless hearts, know that He does."

~CLINT

"My first exposure to 'Rachel's Song' was from my radio. Many people had phoned in for the name of the song. I had a chance to hear it and write it down. When I bought the tape, I rushed home, and as I listened, I cried—a beautiful cry, a peaceful cry. I felt so blessed to be able to hear and enjoy your beautiful composition. I know that God gives special people a priceless talent—and some of us the ability to cherish and enjoy that talent. Thank you."

~MADELYN

"One late afternoon in the spring of 1989, I first heard 'Rachel's Song' as I was sitting in a friend's living room. We were both discussing our desire to start a family, and our lack of success, despite the extensive medical treatment we had both undertaken. 'Rachel's Song' especially touched me. It seemed to be such a happy song, and coupled with the beautiful spring day and the flowers all in bloom, I left my friend with a renewed spirit of determination. On the way home, I stopped and purchased the recording. After reading the story behind the composition of 'Rachel's

Song,' I was sure it was a good omen. All through that summer I listened to the recording. In September, my husband and I decided to pursue adoption. After more heartbreaks and several leads which fell through, we received a phone call the next June. At her christening in September, we too played 'Rachel's Song.' Now, as we begin to pursue another adoption, I again find myself listening over and over again to 'Rachel's Song,' hoping it will again be a good omen. Someday, I will share with my daughter the reason she hears this recording so often. I wanted to share with you how much your music has meant to me."

~JEANNE

"I wanted you to know something about your 'Rachel's Song.' One of my friends is the director of a home for underprivileged children— poor, abused, hyperactive, etc. In any case, she says 'Rachel's Song' is the only one—the only song of any tape—they will sit still and really listen to. I think that's special."

~MARY

"I hadn't played the piano since my husband died. Eight years ago, I married another wonderful man, and he asked me to play the piano many times. I never felt like it until I heard 'Rachel's Song'—but that is one of the most beautiful songs I have ever heard in my life. Now, thanks to you I'm enjoying my piano again. My mother is in a nursing home/rehabilitation center. She is eighty-eight years old. Her birthday is coming up pretty soon. Today, I thanked her again for all those music lessons when I was a kid and told her before she is eighty-nine, I'll play 'Rachel's Song' for her. She was thrilled. She'll have the entire ward in their wheelchairs sitting around the piano the minute I start to play...so I guess I'd better go practice!!!! May God bless."

~JOY

"My office is located in an industrial area. I look out at a lot of concrete and traffic. We have a tremendously high crime rate as well. When I hear your music, I am transported in spirit, heart, and soul to my

safe place in the cool, dry, serene mountains. Thank you for sharing your talent. If every newborn infant in every part of the world had your music as their first sound heard, then I truly believe world peace could be achieved, in time. May you enjoy a bountiful and long life. Respectfully and admiringly yours..."
~Mrs. Lacoure

"First let me say how very much I am enjoying your instrumental album, 'Rachel's Song.' We had a baby, Rachel, born into our family three days ago, and it seems only fitting that she has this beautiful music to wrap herself in as she naps and grows into childhood."
~A family from North Carolina

"I am writing to thank you for 'Rachel's Song.' I am grateful to God for all the beautiful gifts in my life and now for this tape. I belong to a prayer group, and I am anxious to play your music and would like to share Rachel's story. Thank you for the beautiful gift of your music. I feel a strong desire to know more of your music. I have been playing it constantly. I look forward to more. It is truly inspired and inspires me. Thank you again for sharing your gift. Love and peace..."
~Marva

"My wife and I lost our first and only precious daughter Rachel in 1990. She died at birth. We were in our thirties. We were devastated—to go into a hospital with so much hope and love and to come away with so much hurt and pain. We are Christians and leaned so heavily on God. Thank God for our adopted son who was three years old but was God's pillow when we hit the concrete of sorrow. It was only a couple of days, when coming home we heard 'the song' on the radio in the car. We looked at each other like it was Rachel trying to reach us through music. It really was like she was reaching out to us. Telling us to be calm. Peace be with you. Then we heard the radio DJ say very calmly and peacefully, 'You have been listening to Rachel's Song.' We were floored. We had to almost stop the car, we were crying so hard.

We called the radio station. The DJ was so nice, sent us an album of David Combs's music with 'Rachel's Song' on it. It has been a refuge of peace, a resting place for our souls, a connection to our Rachel. We plan to give a CD to our niece, Rachel, and let her know God made this song just for her...just like our Rachel. We love you, David, for allowing God's spirit to write this most beautiful of songs."
~Steve and Marlene

"I have really enjoyed using your music for my kindergartners rest time. They settle down—and there is peace and quiet for an hour. As soon as I begin the music, they curl up on their towels. I also enjoy listening to it in my car. My husband and children have enjoyed it, too. It helps us all to appreciate piano music more. In fact, my daughter has asked to take piano lessons again. Thank you…"
~Mrs. Greene

"Good morning, David Combs…Angel and I so appreciate the two recordings you sent. Each mealtime with our Bose nearby, we are treated to such therapeutic auditory massage as we've not heard since Perry Como. Our music major son says you are a most gifted composer. Thanks again…"
~Paul Harvey, American Radio Broadcaster and National Treasure (personal letter)

"Had you had dinner at our house last evening, you would have heard pianist Gary Prim playing original music by Dave Combs soft, subtle, beautiful original music so that there are no familiar lyrics to intrude on your revelry or on our conversations…. Start with the one called Quiet Escapes, and eating becomes dining."
~Paul Harvey (as spoken live on air)

Epilogue

*How My Music Has Helped People
During the Pandemic*

As the Covid-19 pandemic started to accelerate in 2020, an executive order by the Governor of North Carolina on April 9 effectively locked down all long-term care facilities. Other governors did the same.

That really hit me hard. The nearly three million residents in assisted living and nursing care facilities all over the country were suddenly confined to their rooms, with no visits allowed from family members. The daily bombardment of news stories about the plight of our senior citizens was depressing. In my heart, I knew that I had to do something.

Prior to my mom's death in 2017, I visited her every day for the two-plus years she lived in a wonderful, assisted living facility—Arbor Acres United Methodist Retirement Community, just minutes from our home in Winston-Salem. I saw firsthand how important socialization and music activities were to her mental and physical well-being. I played "Rachel's Song" and my other music many times for programs for her and her "neighbors."

I could only imagine the levels of stress caused by this sudden pandemic isolation. I knew from both scientific studies and anecdotal evidence from my fans that listening to music like mine could have a powerful, stress-reducing effect. So, I decided to combine my own photography of beautiful flowers and peaceful scenery with my own instrumental piano music. I created several YouTube music videos and then put them into two playlists for healthcare providers: one playlist contained twenty-eight short, one-song-length videos, and one playlist contained four long-playing (over six hours each) videos.

The first place I tried out my new videos was at Arbor Acres, where my mom had lived. Janice Lutz-Vanhoy, director of recreation and wellness, had become a good friend from my years visiting my mom. Janice confirmed that the residents at Arbor Acres were very receptive to my soothing music videos.

Okay, I had a model that I knew worked—as I had hoped it would. *How in the world can I get the word out to the 45,000-plus elder-care facilities all over the United States?* I wondered. I used the same approach I did when trying to find gift shops to play and sell my music—I got busy on the phone. This time, the internet made it easier to find the names and phone numbers. Turns out that there are almost 600 assisted living facilities and over 400 nursing home facilities in North Carolina alone.

Starting with assisted living facilities that had the largest number of beds, I personally called and spoke to the activities directors at over 240 of these facilities. As soon as they learned what I was providing to them for free, they were receptive and appreciative. I emailed the YouTube links to each of them, and in no time started receiving positive feedback. I loved the way one person, Gina, put it: "It was good for my soul."

After about a week of spending hours on the phone with these North Carolina activities directors, I knew that I had to find a more efficient way to get the word to the other thousands of similar facilities across the country. Having lived for a couple of years in Alexandria, Virginia—the association capital of the world—I knew there was a lobbying association for just about anything you can imagine. Sure enough, assisted living and nursing care facilities were no exception. I found both national and state level associations. In three full days, I found and contacted by phone all sixty-six associations in the entire country. Their membership included the more than 45,000 facilities that I needed to reach. Nearly all the associations were helpful in passing along information about my free, stress-reducing music videos to their membership.

Finally, my mission of letting virtually every elder-care facility in the nation know how to freely access and play my soothing, relaxing, and stress-reducing music videos on YouTube for their residents was accomplished. I felt a great sense of satisfaction and relief that this important segment of our population had the ability to also be *touched by the music!*

ACKNOWLEDGMENTS

When I started to write this book, I naively thought that writing all the stories in the book would be the hardest part. Turns out that deciding (and remembering) who all to thank by name for their contribution to my life and to the writing of this book is an even bigger challenge.

Throughout my life there have been many people whose support, inspiration, love, and encouragement have helped me—my parents, family, friends, teachers, co-workers, etc. In this book I shared some of my stories about many of those people. Being the analytical person that I am, I counted, and there are over 140 individual people mentioned by name in this book. It is not possible to list, recall, or even know all the people who have helped me in my amazing life journey. It is with my sincere, heart-felt gratitude that I acknowledge many of those people here.

This book would not have happened were it not for the encouragement and support of my wife and best friend for over 50 years, Linda. It was her idea for me to write down all these dozens of stories. It was Linda who came up with the book title, *Touched by the Music*. Forty years ago, it was Linda who insisted that I write down the music of the song I had written, which later was named "Rachel's Song." Now that I think about it, most of the good ideas in our family have originated with her. She is the personification of unconditional love. Over the course of the last year of writing, I have been at times, shall we say, a little grumpy, testy, or just stressed out. Writing a book is hard work. Yet, through it all she has been my rock. I love her to the moon and back.

I am eternally thankful I had the opportunity to play my first song at the Christening service of a beautiful baby girl named Rachel (who will remain anonymous for privacy reasons) where I dedicated this song in her honor.

I am forever grateful to Jack Canfield for his confidence in my writing, his encouragement to me to tell my stories, his willingness to write the Foreword to my book, and for being a true friend. And thanks too to Patty Aubery, Jack's business partner, for her unwavering support.

I especially want to thank Steve Harrison and his amazing team of writing and publishing coaches at Bradley Communications for countless hours of guiding me through the maze of getting my book written, published, and publicized. Thank you master storyteller, Geoffrey Berwind, for teaching me the best ways to craft my stories.

Weaving my numerous stories together into the fabric of my book was a huge challenge. My two editors, Scott and Jocelyn Carbonara, took on this challenge and were enormously helpful.

All through the months of writing this book, anytime I needed that extra special advice or just to hear the positive, uplifting voice of a loving friend, I would call Berry Fowler. Berry's enthusiasm, energy, creativity, business savvy, and attitude of serving and giving are off the charts. His unwavering belief in my book means so much to me.

Linda and I are blessed with many friends, who also volunteered to be advanced readers for this book. Thank you, Barbara and Aubrey Smith, Dan and Sara Underwood, and Garlene Grogan, whom we have known for over forty years. And to my dear friend, Kay Borkowski, thank you for the hours you spent helping me find and use just the right words to make my book both grammatically correct and more easily readable.

Still yet, there are unnamed loyal supporters and fans, over 50,000 of you, who have truly blessed my life. I'm honored each day to receive and read your own amazing notes and stories of how you have been "touched by the music." To each of you, I offer my sincere appreciation and my deepest respect.

Following is a list in alphabetical order of each person to be found somewhere in my book. Thank you for your contribution to my life.

Yolanda Adams, Pat (Uncle Pat) Alderman, Dr. Einar and Susan Anderson, The Association, Patty Aubery, Jim Bailiff, Angi Bemiss, George Benson, Geoffrey Berwind, Frank and Kay Borkowski, Benny Bowes, Cubby Broccoli, Senator James and Louise Broyhill, President

George H. W. Bush, President George W. Bush, Tony Butala, Jack Canfield, Scott Carbonara, Jocelyn Carbonara, Jamie Carter, Jim and Edith Carter, Rachel Carter, Scott Charbo, Dr. James Clark, George Clinton, Uncle Paul & Aunt Phyllis Combs, Joe Combs (my father), Don and Chris Combs (my brother and sister-in-law), Grandmother Combs, Linda Combs (my wife), Ruth Combs (my mother), Claiborn Crain, Jane Crawford (owner of America! gift shop), Harold E. "Doc" Daugherty, Betsy DeGraff, Rev. Gerald Derstine, Jim Doyle, C. H. Duncan, Bill Fleenor, Buck and Jean Foster, Berry Fowler, Sally Fox, Leonard Gallimore, Rob Gerlach, Phil Graham, Preacher and Mrs. Green, Garlene Grogan, Bruce Grubb, Dick Guttman, Phyllis Hall (Bee Separk's daughter), Ed & Lucille Hammer, Bob Handly, Jane Handly, Teresa Harlow, Steve Harrison, Paul Harvey, Governor James Holshouser, David Holt, Jerry Hughes, Carmen Humphrey, Governor James Hunt, Mark Jacoby, Lin Taylor Johnson, Stan Johnson, Chad Kling, Randy Kling, Joe Lacina, Donna Lanier, Johnny Lauffer, Gene Lawson, Jonathon Lee, Hilda Legg, Leslie (co-worker in Maryland), The Lettermen, Ronny Light, Lloyd Lindroth, Jim Loots, Kathy Loots, Janice Lutz-Vanhoy, Ray Lynch, Dottie Martin, Governor James Martin, Bob McHone, Don McLean, Roberta Messner, Doris Miller, Carmon Moon, Stan Moon, Robert & Vera Morrison (Linda's parents), Deputy Secretary Jim Moseley, Cornelia Laemmli Orth, Billy Orton, Alan Packer, Laura Packer, Drew and Marlene Parker, Peter Perret, Dolly Parton, Lewis Phillips, Stephen Plate, Bobby Poynton, Bill Price, Gary Prim, Julie Prim, Phil Pritchard, Ken Raschke, Mrs. Reznick, Elaine Richey, Evan Richey, Russell Riegler, Loudene & Paul Riggs, Hargus "Pig" Robbins, Steve Robertson, Mr. Anthony Rossi, Squire Rushnell, Senator Terry Sanford, Glen Scott, Governor Robert Scott, Mrs. Bee Separk, Harold Shedd, Barbara Smith, Barbara & Aubrey Smith, Cristina Smith, Jana Stanfield, Dr. Fred Tanner, Tant family, Donovan Tea, Three Dollar, Patrick Tucker, Dan & Sara Underwood, Art Unsworth, Rob Van Camp, Secretary Ann Veneman, Betty Wade, Charles Walker, Miles and Pauletta Warfford, Jane Wilkes, Hank Williams, Bill Wood, Eldora Wood, Bob Yesbek

Linda and I are blessed with many friends, who also volunteered to be advanced readers for this book. Thank you, Barbara and Aubrey Smith, Dan and Sara Underwood, and Garlene Grogan, whom we have known for over forty years. Dear friends Bob & Jane Handly, both gifted authors and speakers, thank you for your always sage advice. And to my dear friend, Kay Borkowski, thank you for the hours you spent helping me find and use just the right words to make my book both grammatically correct and more easily readable.

As I was nearing the finish line on publishing this book I was deeply saddened by the passing of our dear friend, Jeanne Robertson, who just weeks before had graciously written the endorsement which is printed on the back cover of this book. Her sense of humor is legendary. Memories of her friendship and love will last forever.

Still yet, there are unnamed loyal supporters and fans, over 50,000 of you, who have truly blessed my life. I'm honored each day to receive and read your own amazing notes and stories of how you have been "touched by the music." To each of you, I offer my sincere appreciation and my deepest respect.

About the Author

DAVE COMBS
Songwriter, Photographer, Author

Dave Combs grew up in Erwin, Tennessee, a small town in upper East Tennessee where music is an important part of the local culture. Dave's family enjoyed making music and taking photographs. Both of his parents and his Grandmother Combs played the piano. So, if Dave's hands were not busy playing the piano, they were often holding an early Kodak box camera or admiring beautiful photos in a National Geographic magazine. While in college, Dave took an aerial photography course, further stimulating and broadening his interest in photography, particularly 3-D photography. Also, during his college years, if Dave wasn't working at his job in the University computer center, he could often be found in one of the practice rooms in the music department playing the piano. He sang in the University Choir, and served as choir director for Calvary Baptist Church, his home church in Erwin.

After receiving his BS degree in Mathematics in 1969 from East Tennessee State University, he moved to Winston-Salem, North Carolina, to begin his twenty-two-year career in information technology at Western Electric/AT&T Network Systems. Soon afterward he met and married his wonderful wife, Linda. Dave served as Minister of Music at Bethany Baptist Church in Winston-Salem. In the mid-70's Dave earned his Master of Business Administration (MBA) graduate degree from

Wake Forest University. He concluded his professional career with five years of service as the Chief Information Officer of the United States Department of Agriculture in Washington, DC.

Dave's first musical composition, "Rachel's Song," was written in 1981, recorded by Gary Prim in 1986, and continues to be a popular instrumental standard around the world. Since that time, Dave has written and produced fifteen instrumental albums of beautiful and inspiring melodies including original compositions, favorite hymns, Christmas music, patriotic music, and other well-known popular songs. For those who play the piano, Dave has transcribed note-for-note and published eleven piano music books from his recordings. Call Combs Music at 800-932-6627 or visit the Combs Music website for more info about these spiral-bound piano music books. Pdf versions of these books as well as the individual songs can be purchased and instantly downloaded from the Sheet Music Plus website, sheetmusicplus.com, under the publisher's name, David M. Combs.

An article, "Two Part Harmony," written by Dave about how music changed his life and touched the lives of millions of people appeared in the September 1994 issue of Guideposts magazine, with a circulation of over two million. Within just a few days, Dave received letters and phone calls from over 10,000 people in response to the article. This article changed his life. A complete reprint of this article is on his website, CombsMusic.com. Eventually, he heard from over 50,000 fans all over the world, filling over 20 large scrapbooks with selected special letters and notes.

His music continues to be played on radio stations, satellite radio, internet radio, and all the streaming music media such as Pandora, Spotify, and iHeart Radio. Dave's music videos can be viewed on his YouTube channel, combsmusic. His CDs can be found on Amazon.com under the artist's name, Gary Prim, and of course at his own website, CombsMusic.com. Digital versions of his music recordings can be purchased and downloaded over the Internet at Amazon.com, iTunes, and Apple Music.

Touched by the Music is Dave's first book. In the book Dave recounts many of the stories of his journey from one song, "Rachel's Song", to fifteen albums of music and eleven piano sheet music books, and the millions of lives that have been touched by his music.

Dave and his wife, Linda, have been supporting charitable organizations for many years including funding scholarships at Appalachian State University, Wake Forest University, and East Tennessee State University. They make their home in Winston-Salem, North Carolina.

Where and How to Find the Music

 The short answer is, go to **CombsMusic.com**. Here is what you will find:

Combs Music recordings and sheet music are available in several forms from several different sources. **Recorded music** is available for purchase on CDs as well as digital downloads. Recordings can also be **streamed** on virtually all streaming media sites and apps by searching for artist, **Gary Prim**. **Sheet music** is available for purchase as printed, spiral bound books as well as instantly available pdf downloads of either single songs or entire albums. **Music videos** with Dave Combs' photography and music can be viewed on YouTube. You can also follow Dave and his music on social media.

Here is a listing of the 15 albums from Combs Music:

Original Composition Instrumental Albums:

Rachel's Song

Beautiful Thoughts

Springtime Reflections

Mellow Moments

Quiet Escapes

Discover Tranquility

Soft Touch

The Outer Banks

Favorite Songs by Other Composers:

Familiar Favorites

Favorite Hymns Instrumental Albums:
September Psalm
Peaceful Praise
Inspirational Treasures

Christmas Instrumental Album:
First Christmas

One Complete Song from each of the other 14 albums:
Combs Music Collection

Here is a listing of the 11 piano music books from Combs Music:

Rachel's Song
Beautiful Thoughts
Springtime Reflections
Mellow Moments
Quiet Escapes
Discover Tranquility
Soft Touch
September Psalm
Peaceful Praise
Inspirational Treasures
First Christmas

Patriotic Instrumental Album (sheet music for selected songs available):
Celebrate Freedom